HEIRLOOM LOVE

Authentic Christianity in This Age of Persecution

Dominic Sputo
with Brian Smith

ISBN 978-0-9907911-4-0 (publication pending)

Contents

WEEK FOUR: LOVE TESTED

WEEK FIVE: LOVE REVIVED

WEEK SIX: LOVE PROVEN

WEEK ONE

Love Lost

"I know all the things you do. I have seen your hard work and your patient endurance. . . . But I have this complaint against you. You don't love me or each other as you did at first!"

—Jesus to the Ephesian church, Revelation 2:2, 4 (NLT)

Week One

Day 1

The Secret Sauce

Use the following link to watch a two-minute video introduction to *Heirloom Love:*

LumenLife.org/hlvideos

We can learn a lot about love from tomatoes.

Maybe I'd better explain. Go back with me two generations.

My grandparents were born and raised in Italy. They entered the US through Ellis Island and settled in New York City. I have a lot of great memories of them. They never learned English. My grandfather made his own wine by stomping grapes in his apartment bathtub. My fondest memory, although intimidating at the time, was of my grandmother right in my face, pinching my cheek and saying in a loud, threatening voice, *"Mangia."* Which I interpreted to mean, "Eat, or else." I affectionately blame her for my adult propensity for overeating.

With this background, I became a foodie before it was trendy. I grew up a foodie just because that's what Italians do: We take food to heart. That's how we share the love. And we shared a lot of love.

When my parents married, they moved from the city to Long Island. My mother's first priority in suburbia was to plant a garden and grow tomatoes.

To understand my mother's priorities, you have to know that although we ate great Italian food every day, the Sunday meal was always the family gem, the crowning culinary achievement to which we always looked forward. It was also typically our simplest meal. And it was always the same—pasta with homemade tomato sauce. Every Sunday, without exception. My mother's Sunday sauce recipe had been handed down through the generations; it was beyond compare.

The secret to my mother's Sunday sauce was, as you may have guessed, the tomatoes. My mother's tomatoes were irresistible. We couldn't wait to eat them. We used to take a salt shaker out to her garden and eat them right off the vine. My mother's home-grown strain were very different from the tomatoes you find in today's grocery stores.

You see, in an effort to come up with the perfect tomato, the agricultural industry has modified God's design for the fruit. They have selectively bred tomatoes for several desirable traits—especially redness (the original stock come in a variety of colors), roundness (versus innumerable odd and even ugly shapes), and firmer texture for durability during transportation and handling. Thanks to science, we now have great looking tomatoes in our markets. Unfortunately, somewhere along the way they lost the *flavor*. The engineered varieties taste bland and indistinct in comparison to their ancestors. Fortunately for the taste buds of humanity, some of the older, truly flavorful strains have been preserved. These are known as heirloom tomatoes, and if you've never tasted one, you literally don't know what you're missing. If you've grown up eating only the most recent strains—whether store-bought or home-grown—you have no idea how good God's tomatoes should taste. Tomatoes didn't lose their flavor overnight. Because the changes were introduced gradually over many years, even I, who experienced the real deal as a child, was fooled and didn't realize that they had lost their flavor until recently when I tasted an heirloom tomato for the first time in many years.

LOVE LIKE TOMATOES?

The love practiced by many in American Christianity seems to have fallen to a fate similar to that of tomatoes. Some say that we've modified God's design, that the fruit has lost its irresistible flavor. Has our Christian love become bland and indistinct in comparison to that of our early church ancestors? Have we lost the distinctive savory essence that Jesus said would cause all men to know that He is the Son of God and that we are His disciples? (See John 13:34–35; also 17:21–23.) For those who answer yes to these questions, there is hope.

Has our Christian love become bland and indistinct in comparison to that of our early church ancestors?

Fortunately, the seeds of heirloom love have been preserved in the Scriptures. Today we can regrow and produce authentic love by learning it from God's Word. If you have never tasted heirloom love, you truly don't know what you're missing. If you've tasted only twenty-first-century Western love, you have no idea how good God's design for Christian love should taste. Until you taste heirloom love, you can't appreciate God's world-winning flavor. It's literally out of this world. The original love strain was irresistible. It was so flavorful that people were coming to Christ even during times of intense persecution (see Philippians 1:28–30; 1 Thessalonians 1:5–7; 2 Corinthians 1:6–7). They were willing to follow Jesus even if it meant losing their loved ones, their livelihoods and their very lives. In comparison, today we go to great lengths to woo people into the front door of a church, but in many cases there are just as many or more walking out the back door. Could it be that the seekers don't taste and see something worth living for—let alone dying for? Might the problem be rooted in our love?

Jesus foresaw and earnestly warned against tasteless Christianity: "You are the salt of the earth. But if the salt loses its saltiness, how can it be made salty again? It is no longer good for anything, except to be thrown out and trampled by men" (Matthew 5:13).

Yet less than a century later some Christians had begun to exercise flavorless "love." When Jesus confronted the Ephesian church, He said that they had forsaken their first love. Even though the Ephesians were known for good works, for perseverance and for hating evil, Jesus was primarily concerned with their lost love, and He sternly warned them (and us) to return to it (see Revelation 2:1–7).

And nearly two thousand years later, a similar strain of man-engineered "love" has taken root in American Christianity. We think we know love, but when we read the New Testament carefully and honestly, we discover that today's "love" is very different from the early church love that changed the world. We are familiar with the New Testament passages on love, but we seem to have lost the Lord's intended meaning and the application practiced by the first believers.

We must return to the original seed. This book is about restoring heirloom love. The love that Jesus and His apostles taught, the love that the thriving early church practiced eagerly and passionately.

Zoom

- Schedule
- Label meeting
  (recurring?)

- generate autom.
  au
  Video - host/
           Participants

Telephone/computer
                audio

Advanced options:
        enable waiting room

Copy invitation

"Taste and see that the Lord is good...."
PSALM 34:8 NIV

Seemingly few Western Christians today are familiar with the taste of heirloom love. It's time to reconsider what Jesus meant when He uttered His "new command": "Love one another. As I have loved you, so you must love one another. By this all men will know that you are my disciples, if you love one another" (John 13:34–35).

These days my family doesn't enjoy pasta with sauce every Sunday, but when we do, it's exciting and we all look forward to it with eager anticipation. But even then, we make it with canned, tasteless tomatoes. If we want the authentic original, like that which my mother used to make, we have to start by growing our own tomatoes from heirloom seeds. Then I can say to my own children, "Taste this and see what you've been missing."

I invite every reader to taste heirloom love. Return with me to the early church in Scripture—to the teachings on love and to the people whose stories exemplify authentic love. Be prepared to challenge your assumptions about love.

What have we been missing?

1. Describe one great example of love you've seen. How was this like (or unlike) the love of Jesus in the Bible?

Week One

Day 2

In Search of Authentic Christianity

A few years ago the Lord disciplined me with an incurable disease, and I literally wasted away to the point of death. In short, I was unfaithful with a large amount of money that the Lord had entrusted to me when a technology company that I started with two friends merged with another company and went public on NASDAQ. The status of money and the material things had lured my heart away from the Lord, and it almost cost me my life.

As I prepared to die, I was forced to acknowledge the worthlessness of this world's attractions when compared to treasure of lasting value. And since that was the Lord's purpose for my illness, He miraculously healed me.

The Lord then led me to create a plan for using His money. So I started studying what the Bible says about money and giving.

In my search for truth I counted 545 verses in the New Testament that directly pertain to money and giving (see Appendix A). Of these verses, 119 deal with general stewardship principles and do not discuss specific purposes for giving. The remaining 426 verses do reveal God's purposes for our giving, and the resulting list of purposes is surprisingly simple. It includes only three categories of beneficiaries for biblical giving:

- 281 verses (66 percent) are specifically related to financially helping poor, suffering and persecuted Christians—that is, our brothers and sisters in the Lord, not "the needy" in general.[1]

- 88 verses (21 percent) pertain to financially helping "the poor" without distinction between Christians and non-Christians.

- 57 verses (13 percent) specifically apply to financially supporting gospel workers, such as missionaries, church pastors and elders.

I was surprised to learn that two-thirds of the New Testament references specifying recipients of our giving pertain to helping persecuted and suffering Christians. In hindsight, I should not have been surprised. After all, we know from 1 Corinthians 16:1–2 that the apostle Paul originally initiated Sunday collections specifically to collect money for suffering Christians: "Now concerning the collection for the saints, as I have given orders to the churches of Galatia, so you must do also: On the first day of the week let each one of you lay something aside, storing up as he may prosper, that there be no collections when I come" (NKJV).

The first and only record of Sunday collections in the New Testament says they were designated 100 percent for aid to suffering Christians living in a foreign land. Contrast that with American Christianity where it is estimated that less than one-half of 1 percent of our Sunday collections are used to help persecuted Christians. How can this be? Paul was unmistakably clear that caring for suffering Christians isn't optional.—he issued "orders" to this effect.

Paul was unmistakably clear that caring for suffering Christians isn't optional.

Yes, I understand that first-century believers also gave offerings for other legitimate purposes, and I am not suggesting that today's church budgets should be 100 percent designated to suffering Christians. My point is to highlight the huge shift in values and priorities. The early church provided aid to persecuted Christians as one

---

[1] Some of these verses do not specifically indicate why the Christians in these passages were suffering or in need. However, because persecution is almost continuously an understood part of the New Testament context, these Scriptures likely refer to Christians who were suffering and in need due to persecution. Biblical references to "the poor" and "the needy" refer to people who are suffering and perishing because they do not have daily food or other basic resources necessary to sustain life (see, for example, Luke 3:11; James 2:15–16).

of their highest priorities. In sharp contrast, American Christians are culpable of near-complete neglect of our most needy family, even though both the need and the available resources are much greater today.

Neither am I suggesting we should give 66 percent of our offerings to suffering and persecuted Christians, 21 percent to the poor, and 13 percent to gospel workers (proportional to the number of New Testament verses in each category). However, if preponderance of mention is any indicator of importance to the Lord (and I believe it is), then helping persecuted and suffering Christians should be our highest priority, or one of our highest.

THE STATE OF THE CHURCH

After reading these passages and the many other related Scriptures presented in this book, my family and I understood that we needed to help persecuted Christians. So we searched for churches and church-based organizations through whom we could send an offering to help them. We ended up contacting the leaders of the 150 largest Christian churches and the twenty largest Christian denominational organizations. Here is what we learned:

Sadly, only two of the denominations and three of the churches indicated that they include their persecuted brothers and sisters in their ministry purpose and plan. Of these five organizations, only one made this ministry a significant budgetary item. Eight others indicated that they sometimes, albeit infrequently, provide assistance to persecuted Christians.

The truth is that the leading Christian churches and denominations in the wealthiest nation on earth are ignoring the plight of their suffering brothers and sisters. Such negligence is contrary to Scripture, where we see that financially assisting the saints in tribulation is the dominant theme of New Testament giving. You will see this borne out as you study the Bible passages referenced throughout this book.

1. **What was your first impression upon learning that:**

Financially helping suffering and persecuted Christians is the most-often-mentioned purpose of New Testament giving?

Very few American Christians remember their persecuted brothers and sisters?

2. **With so few American Christians helping, and less than one-half of 1 percent of American church collections being used to aid persecuted Christians, how does this affect the credibility of American Christianity and our ability to influence and change our culture (see John 13:34–35; 17:21–23)?**

Week One

Day 3

Missing in Inaction

Many believers today do not understand the biblical mandate and priority to help the persecuted saints because the relevant Scriptures are often read and taught without consideration of their context. Consequently, many American Christians have either misunderstood or forgotten their original meaning and application.

Take, for example, 2 Corinthians 8–9, which we'll dig into in Week Three. This passage is the most significant and substantive teaching and example of giving in the New Testament. Leaders use it so broadly, asking for money for many causes, that we're apt to misunderstand or forget that it was written to raise financial support for suffering and persecuted Christians in a foreign land.

This is only one of numerous relevant New Testament examples and admonitions to care for persecuted fellow believers. Persecution was a major concern for the first-century church. It's far worse today! We're living in a time when more Christians are being martyred, tortured, incarcerated and oppressed for Christ's sake than ever before.

Experts disagree sharply on the number of Christians who are killed for their faith every year. Their estimates range from several thousand on the low end to more than one hundred thousand—brothers and sisters murdered every year simply because they love Jesus. The numbers vary primarily because experts disagree in their definitions of what constitutes a Christian and when murder constitutes martyrdom. The exact number isn't important for our purpose in this book. Regardless of how you define martyrdom, an estimated two hundred million Christians are, at this very moment, suffering greatly in many other ways for Christ's name's sake.

An estimated two hundred million Christians are, at this very moment, suffering greatly for Christ's name's sake.

The church of Jesus is suffering as much as—if not more than—it ever has. That's why the New Testament's teachings on helping persecuted believers are as critically relevant today as when they were first written.

INFORMATION UNDERLOAD

You might be wondering, *If Christians are being persecuted and murdered on such a cruel and massive scale, why don't we know it?*

Except for recent reporting about ISIS (Islamic State in Iraq and Syria), mainstream media and most politicians have ignored virtually all the horrific news about Christian persecution. When secular media sources do report on situations involving Christian persecution, they often hide the truth by inaccurately and vaguely describing such events as "terrorism" or "tribal," "sectarian" or "political" conflicts, rather than attacks on Christians. Even many US church leaders avoid talking about persecution for fear of jeopardizing their multicultural evangelistic initiatives, or because it is "a downer," according to a Barna Research Associates survey of American pastors.[2] Although Christian persecution is the most pervasive and severe violation of human rights in the world, so few people—even Christians in the US, with our access to information—know much about it.

Because mainstream news sources report tragedies like the ongoing massacre in Nigeria as merely "terrorism" or "sectarian violence," most American Christians do not know that an estimated forty thousand people, mostly Christians, have been

---

[2] Carl Moeller, "Millions Are Persecuted, and the Church Wants to Know," ChristianHeadlines.com, October 21, 2011, christianheadlines.com/news/millions-persecuted -church-wants-toknow.html.

brutally murdered in northern Nigeria since Sharia law was instituted in 2010. Or that 2.5 million—mostly Christians—are now homeless because of violence or threats of violence against them.

We can't rely on mainstream secular media or many of our politicians to provide us with accurate and complete persecution-related news. Persecution news is available to a limited degree on the Internet. However, most Christian persecution is never reported because local authorities often sympathize with the persecutors and refuse to assist Christians or allow their stories to be made known. Local officials often subject Christians to further oppression when they cry out and seek help from the outside world.

Still, the reliable news sources we *do* have provide us with ample evidence that a staggering number of our spiritual family members around the globe are being severely mistreated for loving Jesus.

1. **Use your imagination to stir your heart for our persecuted family. In your mind, build a picture—as real as possible—of yourself and your loved ones in the following circumstances:**

    - Because you and your loved ones follow Jesus, many people in your community begin to spread false rumors, accusing Christians—and you, specifically—of immoral behavior, dishonesty, and even crimes.

    - Government agencies begin to demand new "fees" for electricity, water, and other services, sometimes "accidentally" interrupting service and taking days to restore it. Police begin following your family members. Local officials threaten consequences unless you "come to your senses."

    - Your business loses customers, or you are fired from your job. Your family struggles to survive on less income. Neighbors and extended family, upon whom you thought you could rely for help, now snub you.

    - Various possessions—jewelry, tools, the car, your pet—go mysteriously missing. Christian women—maybe you, your wife, your mother, your daughter—while shopping or walking to school or work, are increasingly subjected to sexual harassment. One is kidnapped and raped.

    - One day a violent mob—or maybe the police—knock on your door and force your family to leave your home. You grab any valuables you can, flee into the street, and watch as your home is burned to the ground.

    - Desperate, you find a "camp" with other homeless people, including an increasing number of Christians. Maybe it's in a nearby forest, sheltering under windblown tarps. Maybe it's in a garbage dump.

- One of your loved ones fails to come home from foraging one day. You learn that he (or she) has been arrested on false charges, and his captors are torturing him for a confession. After days of futile pleas, you receive your loved one back, and you tend to his wounded body and spirit as well as you can. He's not the same.

- As weeks and months pass, more cold, hungry Jesus followers join your camp. More are arrested, imprisoned and tortured. Some never return. You pray constantly for rescue—not just for yourself, but for innocent children and frail elders, all dear to you. You learn new strength in trusting and loving the Lord, and in loving people who are worse off than you. But your circumstances only decline. Day after interminable day.

Given these circumstances for millions of Christians today, what do you think they wish they could tell you? If you were in the situation described above, and you could send a letter to a Christian living in a free, prosperous country, what would you say? Write three to five sentences to share with your group.

2. Watch the three-minute video at *LumenLife.org/FrancisChan*. What impresses you about Francis Chan's heart for the persecuted church?

Week One

Day 4

Nothing New Under the Sun

Equipped with awareness of the widespread persecution of Christians, what then is our obligation before God?

It's the same as it was two thousand years ago, at a time when "heirloom love" was simply known as . . . love.

SAME SITUATION, DIFFERENT DAY

They went on stoning Stephen . . . . And on that day a great persecution began against the church in Jerusalem, and they were all scattered throughout the regions of Judea and Samaria, except the apostles. (Acts 7:59; 8:1, NASB)

After Stephen was murdered, people throughout Jerusalem took up arms against the followers of Jesus.

According to clues in Acts, there were likely ten thousand or more adult believers in Jesus by the time of Stephen's martyrdom.[3]Imagine the multiple hardships implied when we read that "they were all scattered" throughout the surrounding regions. Fleeing for their lives, perhaps tens of thousands of people, including children, left behind their homes, their livelihoods, their extended families and support networks. Today in the West, we can fall back on temporary housing and on help to find new employment. But these people literally faced a

---

[3] See Acts 2:41, 47; 4:4; 5:14; 6:1, 7.

life-and-death quandary as they attempted to resettle in strange lands. Who would come to their aid? The uncaring Roman government? No. The majority of fellow Jews, who disbelieved the claims of Jesus? No. They were dependent solely on the mercy of other Jesus followers to provide them with food and shelter.

It's in this context that we're meant to read the New Testament admonitions to hospitality—specifically for the sake of Jesus' homeless followers who were being persecuted for loving Him: "Do not neglect to show hospitality to strangers, for by this some have entertained angels without knowing it" (Hebrews 13:2, NASB). And, "Offer hospitality to one another without grumbling" (1 Peter 4:9).

Do not neglect to show hospitality to strangers, for by this some have entertained angels without knowing it.

Commands such as these were written specifically to exhort the more fortunate believers to provide life-sustaining aid to Christian refugees who had been driven from their homes by persecution. Let's be careful not to redefine or minimize these teachings to mean merely having friends over for dinner.

FROM THE ENDS OF THE EARTH

So if a persecuted Christian knocks at my door, God commands me to help him or her. But you're talking about persecuted Christians on the other side of the world.

Yes, you're right. The first line of aid for the Jerusalem refugees was the believers in the regions to which they fled—Judea and Samaria. But the Church, the one unified body of Christ, is much larger, and Jesus intends that His worldwide Church come to the aid of His suffering people.

"The disciples were called Christians first at Antioch. . . . The disciples, each according to his ability, decided to provide help for the brothers living in Judea. This they did, sending their gift to the elders by Barnabas and Saul" (Acts 11:26, 29–30). The regions of Judea and Samaria were within two or three days' travel of Jerusalem. Antioch, on the other hand, was three hundred miles to the north—a good two-week journey. This was nowhere in the neighborhood. In fact, sending a financial gift today from the United States to any other point in the world is much easier than it was for Barnabas and Saul to carry this gift three hundred miles from Antioch to Jerusalem. And the Christians of Antioch were much less likely ever to meet one of the brothers or sisters they helped than you are to meet a persecuted brother or sister from Asia or Africa. And still they helped. Distance didn't matter. Cultural and linguistic differences didn't count. Only their oneness in Jesus was meaningful, and they did what family does.

Paul is known for numerous "collections for the saints." This was probably the first. Later he would collect money for suffering saints from Christians who lived even farther away—in modern-day Turkey and Greece.[4]

As we will see later, Peter, James and John all gave similar instructions to Christians—to provide for the physical needs of suffering fellow believers.

What about you? What about your church? It's my hope that, because of what I'm sharing, you might reexamine your giving and priorities in the light of the Scriptures presented in this book.

Even a small (and growing) number of committed believers can radically multiply the help that's currently going to our oppressed family.

---

[4] See Romans 15:25–26; 1 Corinthians 16:1; 2 Corinthians 8:1–5.

1. Describe what you imagine what life was like for the first Christian refugee families. What did they lose? How did they survive? From whom could they get help?

2. Considering that the New Testament teachings on hospitality were first intended to benefit persecuted Christian refugees, how might you apply those Bible passages?

Week One

Day 5

Compassion and Grace

1. Based on the Lord's description of King Josiah (Jeremiah 22:16) and of Himself (Exodus 34:5–6), what kind of behavior shows that we truly know God? (Optional: See Matthew14:14; 20:34; Mark 1:41; Luke 7:13.)

2. In your own words, describe the love Jesus taught us to practice in the Luke 10:25–37.

I lived an irresponsible and destructive lifestyle until I was twenty-eight years old. I was drowning in debt, past-due on seemingly countless credit card accounts. Something needed to change in my life, but trying harder to change, I found myself sliding deeper into sin. Lost in the misery of fleshly living, I finally realized my desperate need for grace, to be saved from my sins. With the help of a friend named

Dale, I understood that Christ died to pay the penalty for my wrongs and to set me free from sin so I might live a new life in Him.

Once I became a Christian, God's grace redeemed my past mistakes and gave me clarity for walking in His wisdom. In my zeal for handling money God's way, I decided to give a small amount from each paycheck to my local church. Though it was a mere token, it was significant to me. At the time, the minimum payments on my credit cards totaled more than my income, and creditors were calling me almost daily. Giving an offering of any amount was a sacrifice.

The day after I gave my first offering, I found a large stack of hundred- and fifty-dollar bills that someone had misplaced. I immediately called both my pastor and my best friend, Paul, an attorney, and asked what I should do with the money. They both told me to call the police. Go ahead, nominate me for the "Duh" Award for even needing to ask. But I did need to ask. This was new territory for me. Before Jesus saved me, I would have claimed "finders keepers" and kept the money.

After I called the police, a detective was dispatched to pick up the money and prepare a report. The detective told me they would have to conduct an investigation, and the money would be returned to me if they didn't find the owner within ninety days.

I spent the next ninety days planning how to spend "my" money. I went shopping and picked out a new speedboat and a wardrobe of new clothes. It never occurred to me, despite their frequent phone reminders, that I might use the money to pay my creditors. At the end of the ninety days, I inquired about the money. The detective told me they hadn't started the investigation and it was going to take another ninety days.

On the Sunday after I received this news, my church started a six-week stewardship program. After the second Sunday of this program, I finally understood that all the money in my possession belongs to the Lord, and I'm responsible for using His money to accomplish His purposes. I'm a steward, a manager—not an owner. I vowed that if the police gave the money back to me, I wouldn't spend it without first seeking the Lord's purpose for it.

The next day—yes, the next day—the detective called and said they'd completed the investigation early. The money was mine! After seeking to know the Lord's will for it, I gave an offering to my church and used the remainder to repay my debts. Imagine that! No speedboat or new clothes in the Lord's plan for me!

I was overwhelmed by the Lord's compassion and grace toward me and by His command that we "go and do the same" in our compassion toward others (Luke 10:37, NASB). I made a vow that, if my income increased, I would not increase my consumption or standard of living. Instead, I would use any additional money to express God's compassion to the poor.

It was easy for me to make that commitment, because at that time in my life my wife, Debbie, and I were content with spending less than we were earning. We were living in a modest home, driving modest cars, taking simple vacations, occasionally dining out at inexpensive restaurants, and purchasing only the things we needed. Little did I know that just six months later the Lord was going to put my word to the test—by blessing me. That's when my friends and I started a technology company that became very successful and went public on NASDAQ.

THE GRADUATE SCHOOL OF OBEDIENCE

Money is like an acid test that penetrates our exterior religious veneer and reveals the true condition of our hearts. From firsthand experience, I know this to be true because I failed the test. I sold my stock in our company, and I broke my pledge not to increase my consumption and standard of living. I conveniently adopted the popular teaching that says "ten percent for God and ninety percent for me." I gave ten percent of the stock sale proceeds to my local church—plus an additional ten percent of "my money" to various charities—in an ill-fated attempt to placate my conscience for indulging myself with the remaining eighty percent.

> **Money is like an acid test that penetrates our exterior religious veneer and reveals the true condition of our hearts.**

I fooled myself into believing that I should build a new waterfront home that was five times larger than our previous comfortable home. I tried to convince Debbie that we needed this house "to do the Lord's work," such as hosting Bible studies and outreach activities. Debbie didn't share my vision, so it was against her counsel that I built the house. This was one of the biggest mistakes I've ever made.

Shortly after we moved into our new home, I was bitten by a tick while on a church camping trip. A few days later, I developed a Lyme disease rash, and within two weeks I began to experience other severe symptoms of the disease. I was infected with a particularly aggressive strain that did not respond to antibiotics. My health declined rapidly. Within eighteen months I looked like a walking skeleton. I developed severe arthritis so debilitating that I had great difficulty getting out of bed. My fatigue became so great that walking any distance—even from one side of our home to the other—was a chore. Our spacious new house felt like a curse.

The Lyme disease caused me to forget what I was saying, and I could not finish my sentences. I lost the tissue that padded my seat and the bottoms of my feet, so sitting or standing was painful without pillows and special padding in my shoes. My spine and joints cracked loudly when I moved.

I developed liver complications and candida from excessive antibiotics. The candida caused intestinal and digestion issues, as well as a thick white thrush coating that grew on my tongue and blackish green fungus that grew in my nails. As if I didn't look pitiful enough already, red bumps the size of pencil erasers grew on my head and neck.

Yes, this was the life.

Shortly after I became sick, the Lord revealed to me that the disease was no accident; He was disciplining me for my unfaithfulness with His money (see Hebrews 12:5–11). I had tried to hijack His story and make it about me. So He dragged me kicking and screaming into my own private wilderness that He might have all my attention. He got it. I repented of my unfaithfulness, and the Lord set me free from bondage to money—a counterfeit master who promised to satisfy my soul, but who would betray me every time. The Lord healed me of a spiritual ailment that had harmed me more severely than my physical ailment—it had turned my heart away from Him.

Once again, the joy of the Lord became my strength. Outwardly I continued to waste away, but inwardly I was being renewed day by day.

Just to be clear, I don't believe that every negative circumstance is a sign of the Lord's discipline for sin, nor that every positive circumstance is evidence of His blessing for obedience. Learning to discern the Lord's intention in our circumstances is a matter of prayer, careful consideration and wise counsel.

THE GRACE OF A SECOND CHANCE

My ordeal had now lasted eighteen months. My health continued to deteriorate, and Debbie and I were losing hope. We believed my earthly days were coming to end. I wasted away to the point that my bones were sticking out. Debbie and my mother could hardly look at me without crying.

"I prayed for a second chance"

About this time a sister in the Lord gave me a sermon video and another friend gave me a book—both about boldly and persistently crying out to Lord, with childlike wailing, until He comes to our rescue (see Luke 18:1–8). I was desperate. During the next three weeks, I went to a quiet place where no one else could hear me, and every day I mourned, lamented and wailed loudly, pleading with the Lord to heal me. I literally carried on like a desperate child who was lost in the wilderness, scared and about to die.

After three weeks of crying out, I received a call from a faithful brother in the Lord named Alex. He said the Lord had just told him to call and tell me He was going to heal me. At that moment, the Lord did exactly that! He healed me. Hallelujah! All the Lyme disease symptoms immediately left my body. My memory, liver and digestive issues returned to normal. The red bumps, thrush and fungus disappeared, and I had energy for the first time in eighteen months. I felt like I'd been raised from a living death.

Through my recovery the Lord was telling me, *Your part in My story isn't finished yet, son. I have more for you to do for Me here on earth.* I renewed my resolve to love and serve the Lord with all my heart, soul, mind and strength—and with whatever wealth He entrusted to me. This was the beginning of my journey to finding heirloom love.

* * *

Please note: If you were to read only the Scriptures quoted in this book concerning our responsibility to minister to suffering and persecuted Christians, you could get the impression that salvation can be earned by doing good deeds. However, we know by reading the whole Bible that salvation is by grace, through faith and not by works. Please see Appendix B for a more detailed understanding of salvation by grace through faith.

A NOTE ABOUT REAL LIFE STORIES

I want to caution you before you read the following story—one of several persecution stories you'll read throughout this book. Perhaps I can best illustrate my point by describing a recent experience.

I was invited to speak at a church on the topic of persecution in the Middle East. After I finished, the pastor roused the church to anger against those who persecute Christians. My heart sank in response to his angry tone and words. My message wasn't intended to spotlight evil men, but rather to highlight the circumstances of and encourage compassion for the brothers and sisters in our persecuted family.

Similarly, the stories in this book are presented to encourage you to remember and have compassion for the persecuted body of Christ. If we're not careful, these stories can stir up fear, anger and hate towards those inflicting the harm, as it did to Peter when he cut off Malchus's ear when "defending" Jesus. But the Spirit whispers, "Love your enemies and pray for those who persecute you" (Matthew 5:44). Jesus led the way for us when He was nailed to the cross and prayed, "Father, forgive them, for they do not know what they are doing" (Luke 23:34).

We must continually remind ourselves that "our struggle is not against flesh and blood, but against the rulers, against the authorities, against the powers of this dark world and against the spiritual forces of evil in the heavenly realms" (Ephesians 6:12). Our enemy is not Hinduism, Islam, Communism or Buddhism. Nor is it the people who practice these religions.

There are more stories in this book about persecution in Islamic nations than under any other belief system. This is not due to any bias on my part. It is because twelve out of the top fifteen countries with the worst records for religious persecution are Islamic nations.[5]

---

[5] See "2017 Annual Report," United States Commission on International Religious Freedom, 2017, uscirf.gov/reports-briefs/annual-report/2017-annual-report.

Week One

Day 6

Real Life in Laos

Exiled for Love and Lord[6]

Katin is a peaceful village. Until Jesus invades.

Family by family, one household at a time, a church grows in the highland village in southern Laos. They build a place of worship. They select a pastor. They openly adore their Lord and Savior.

But as Jesus promised, troubles follow soon. Communist Laos is 1.5 percent Christian and 67 percent Buddhist. The rest of the population are mostly animistic spiritists inhabiting outlying areas like the vicinity of Katin. The villagers fear that the Christians' defections from spirit worship will anger the locality's many powerful spirits, bringing upon the whole village any number of illnesses and other calamities. And so this recent wave of local persecution—which continues to our present day—begins in 2003: Government officials confiscate the church building, forcing our brothers and sisters to start meeting outdoors. Three years later the pastor is murdered. The believers persist in worship.

Two years after that, villagers seize a Christian man named Pew and pour rice wine down his throat. He dies of asphyxiation. The grieving family buries their loved one and places a wooden cross upon his grave—an action village officials

---

[6] Sur's perceptions of events are fictionalized, but he and the events portrayed are completely real.

condemn as "practicing the rituals of the enemy of the state." They fine the family by taking their water buffalo and a pig. One pig is a devastating loss, but taking a family's buffalo—their beast of burden—is like confiscating a farmer's tractor.

By this time, twenty families in Katin have come to faith in Christ, but over the next few weeks all of them—threatened with eviction and eventual starvation—give in to pressure and sign documents renouncing their faith.

We don't know whether twelve-year-old Sur watched all this from the safety of an unbelieving home or whether his family was one of those who followed Christ. But he was there. He saw. He knew something of the life-changing power of this god and the man named Jesus.

There are no secrets in a village like Katin, and word gets out that some of the believers have begun gathering again for prayer and worship. Neither God's Holy Spirit nor His people will be suppressed.

After Pew's murder, the previously disinterested district and provincial officials come to the Christians' aid . . . *at the orders of the communist Laotian central government*. The officials visit the village in order to clarify the laws of Laos. In persecuting the Christians, they say, the village leaders have violated the country's constitution, which guarantees freedom of religion. Justice and freedom have finally come to Katin.

But once the officials have performed their required duty, they leave the Christians in the hands of the hostile villagers. Four days later the village authorities seize a Christian family's buffalo, offering to return it if the family will renounce their faith. The father refuses, and the next day the officials slaughter the buffalo and distribute the meat to non-Christian families. They promise to continue seizing livestock until there are no more Christians or no more animals belonging to Christians.

Our brothers and sisters worship on. Over the next two years they endure further dire threats and theft of their livestock. Eventually the village chief declares that only spirit worship is acceptable in his village. By now we know that Sur's family has come to faith in Christ.

This sets the scene for the Sunday that marks the turning point of Sur's life.

Fourteen-year-old Sur gasps and stares, watching a hundred hostile villagers and local officials intrude on the Christian worship service about ten o'clock that Sunday morning. Cold fear grips Sur as guns are placed to the heads of various church members. All forty-eight of them—men, women and children from eleven families—are forced out to an open field.

"Renounce your faith!" demand the village leaders, fearing the wrath of angered spirits over the Christians' worship of Jesus. Something inside Sur wonders if they're right. After all, not long ago his now-Christian family routinely sacrificed to the spirits.

Sur turns his frightened gaze to his father and mother, and he sees the solemn resolve on their faces, bolstered by their love and trust for Jesus. He is still afraid, but he strengthens his determination to mimic their conviction. Maybe if he behaves bravely he'll feel braver. It helps a little. He consciously stands taller as the confrontation continues.

No matter what threats and gibes the village leaders scream at the Christians, none will deny Jesus Christ. They hold dear the love and forgiveness of their Lord and the promise of eternity with Him.

Meanwhile, Sur can hear and see the ransacking of the eleven families' homes. Their belongings are thrown carelessly out onto the ground. The villagers confiscate one family's pig, worth six weeks' labor. And then the worst: Six of the Christians' homes are completely destroyed before their eyes.

Sur looks around at his older brother Yead, younger sister Ngoy, and eight-year-old brother Jeed, and at his other friends and their parents. Many are weeping, watching the pillage and destruction of all they own—wanting to intervene, yet mindful of the weapons trained on them. Death rests in the hands of their enemies.

Finally, when the leaders and officials realize they're not succeeding at dissuading any of the Christians from their faith, they once again point their guns directly at the Christians' heads and command them to begin walking along the road out of the village. The bereft and suddenly destitute families snatch up what belongings they can grab and begin the march to a location four miles away, on the edge of the jungle, where they will establish the new "home" they will inhabit for at least the next two years.

Sur is beginning the ordeal that will impact the rest of his life. He and the other forty-seven believers—including two-year-olds and adults as old as sixty—are abandoned virtually empty-handed at the side of the road.

"You may not come back until you renounce Christ," say the officials.

With growing dread Sur realizes, *We have no food. I need water, now. Is there any water here? We can't protect ourselves. No shelter . . . or tools for building or farming. We need our water buffalo to pull the plow. Wait, we have no plow!*

The small community begins immediately searching for food, water and any form of shelter. They anticipate the rains lasting for two more months. Then the bone-chilling mountain temperatures of Laos's dry winter, with no rainwater—only the tiny, polluted trickle of a nearby stream—until late spring or early summer.

That night, Sur sleeps on the hard ground under the most heavily foliaged tree his family can find. These dear friends enter that dark night "speaking to one another in psalms and hymns and spiritual songs, singing and making melody with [their] heart to the Lord; always giving thanks for all things in the name of our Lord Jesus Christ to God, even the Father" (Ephesians 5:19–20, NASB).

They knew it might happen. And still they stuck with Jesus.

Picture these dear Jesus followers building temporary shelters without the benefit of tools, repeatedly ordered to stop building shelters and to sleep on the ground. They refuse. Under the meager protection of a branches-and-grass struc-ture, Sur tries to ignore his hunger and the whimpering of the community's chil-dren as he shivers in the cold. Does he sometimes wish his family would just reject Jesus? Who could blame him?

Feel these believers' defeat when, days later, the district official turns against them and declares that he will allow no Christianity on his watch. Or the short-lived thrill when the district official is overruled by the provincial governor, who visits the forty-eight at their jungle refuge and assures them they may worship as they wish and live wherever they please.

But it's only words. Nothing changes.

Imagine the physical condition of our brothers and sisters over the next several months—the multiple diseases they contract from eating whatever animal life and edible vegetation they can find in the jungle, from drinking water unfit for inges-tion. For three months they're refused medical treatment, until at last two become so ill that they're allowed hospitalization. Join Sur with his family, huddled in prayer for one of the sick individuals. Feel the bottom drop out of Sur's world as he listens to his father praying, hears his father's labored breathing—then opens his eyes to see his father falter and suddenly die.

The next year and a half is filled with the backs and forths of a spiritual battle turned very physical. Of warfare literally to the death. The families are allowed to retrieve limited quantities of rice from the village, but only enough to stave off complete starvation. Some families return to their hereditary rice fields and begin cultivating, even without buffalos, even though it's off season, just to gain a little extra food and to preserve their right to use the fields under Laotian law. But villagers drain the paddies, burn the protective fences and trample the rice seed-lings; officials prohibit the Christians from returning or replanting their former farmland. So the eleven desperate families begin the laborious process of clearing new farming space near their place of exile; persons unknown burn their seed supply and the few farming tools they've acquired or improvised.

Seven more Katin families come to faith in Jesus Christ—two immediately following the original expulsion, four after the villagers threaten to shoot any returning exiles, and one on the heels of new expulsion threats. These fifteen new believers are cast out of the village and are welcomed by the forty-eight, who build additional shelters and cut their own rations to share with their brothers and sisters in need.

Take a moment to reread that last sentence. And marvel.

In February, more than a year after their eviction from the village, comes the beginning of the dry season.

The exiled Katin Christians, numbering sixty-two, are so utterly defeated they resort to begging for food. Authorities defy their own nation's constitution, circulating word to all nearby villages that no one should help the "lawbreaking" Christians.

By July, the outcasts are still dependent on outside support. But the rains have come, their new fields are growing rice, and their health has greatly improved. Some of the children are allowed to attend school in a nearby township, and more believers are coming out of the Katin village woodwork, quietly visiting the refugees for worship.

September: Five new Katin families have come to faith in Christ, and three of the exiled families return to the village to join them. Village officials can't ignore this; they demand a fine of one pig per family.

At this point we lose word of Sur and the rest of the church at Katin. No further mention of their situation is found in available Internet articles as of the time of this writing.

Katin is only one of hundreds or thousands of variations on the same theme, travesties being perpetrated today against the hundred thousand Christians in Laos—one of the world's worst countries for human rights violations and persecution of Christians.[7]

---

[7] Information for this story was compiled from dozens of reports accessible through World Watch Monitor at worldwatchmonitor.org; Human Rights Watch for Lao Religious Freedom at hrwlrf.net; Mission Network News at mnnonline.org (all accessed during April–June 2013, search terms: *katin laos* via each site's search engine; more recent research has uncovered no new information); and from private letters from unidentifiable sources in country.

Week One Group Discussion Guide

After completing Days 1–5 and reading the real life story, meet with your group and use this discussion guide to help you "spur one another on toward love and good deeds" (Hebrews 10:24). The time allotments are suggestions for a sixty-minute discussion.

PRAY (5 minutes)

Begin by inviting the Lord to fill your hearts with His love, perhaps using Paul's prayer for the Thessalonian church as a model:

May the Lord make your love increase and overflow for each other and for everyone else, just as ours does for you. May he strengthen your hearts so that you will be blameless and holy in the presence of our God and Father when our Lord Jesus comes with all his holy ones. (1 Thessalonians 3:12–13)

SHARE (45 minutes)

Share with the group your thoughts and discoveries from the following questions:

Day 2, questions 1 and 2

Day 3, question 1

Day 4, question 1

Day 5, question 1

Share your thoughts about real life in Laos.

CLOSE: (10 minutes)

Pray for the Christians in Laos. Ask the Lord to:

- Save the Laotian communist leaders.
- Turn the authorities' hearts to allow God's people to worship Him peacefully.
- Keep the Laotian Christians' faith from failing.
- Strengthen and grow His church in Laos.

Pray for yourselves. Ask the Lord to bear fruit from the seeds of His Word, sown in your hearts this week.

Ask for one or two volunteers who will each take a few minutes during the upcoming week to read the latest persecution news and briefly share one or two news stories at your next group meeting. Persecution news is available at *LumenLife.org/news.*

WEEK TWO

Love Found

"A new command I give you: Love one another. As I have loved you, so you must love one another."

—Jesus, John 13:34

Day 1   Love One Another

Day 2   Friends with Jesus

Day 3   Peter's Priority

Day 4   John Defines Authentic Christianity

Day 5   James Describes True Religion

Day 6   Real Life in Eritrea: Worship from a Metal Box

Group Discussion Guide

Week Two

Day 1

Love One Another

Use the following link to watch a one-minute introduction to Week Two of your journey to heirloom love:

LumenLife.org/hlvideos

1. In the Old Testament, the Lord commanded His people to love their neighbors as themselves (see Leviticus 19:18), a command that Jesus reinforced (for example, Matthew 22:36–40). What, then, was new about Jesus' "new command" (John 13:34–35; 15:12–14).

2. Why is it significant that Jesus waited until the Last Supper—His final night with His disciples (John 13:1, 3)—to give them His new command?

What do you do when the Author of the Ten Commandments says, "I have a new commandment for you"?

Think about it. Imagine yourself sitting by Jesus' side on that fateful night when He was about to be arrested and crucified. The Messiah spends the evening with you, sharing His final and most important teachings (John 13–17). And on this evening, among His many teachings and reassurances, Jesus says, "I'm about to give you a new commandment."

What? No one has added to Israel's commandments since the time of Moses! After the first five books—the "Books of Moses"—the rest of the Old Testament serves to clarify, illustrate and interpret the commandments given through Moses. But no new commandments have been added throughout the whole of God's revealed Word.

Until this night.

Tonight the Word Incarnate sits beside you. Just as He did thousands of years ago, when He revealed His heart through His commandments to Israel, so again tonight He speaks. His new command: "Love one another. As I have loved you, so you must love one another" (John 13:34).

This command is the heartbeat we've seemingly lost, the DNA of heirloom love. When it comes to the core teachings that guide the Christian lifestyle, Jesus' new command belongs at the very center. At least, that's what the apostle John seemed to think, as we'll see. And who would know the true heart of the Messiah better than one of His closest friends, one of His inner circle of three, the one to whom Jesus entrusted the care of His mother after His death? It's through John's gospel and his letters that we receive Jesus' new command.

When it comes to the core teachings that guide the Christian lifestyle, Jesus' new command belongs at the very center.

Jesus' new command includes several important implications. First, it's a *command*; His followers, including you and me, are required to obey it. Next, Jesus was commanding us to love "one another"—that is, to love fellow believers. John confirmed this several times in his letter (see 1 John 2:7–11; 3:10–23; 4:20–21). Jesus did not mean to prohibit love for unbelievers. In fact, He taught exactly the opposite (for example, in Matthew 5:43–47). But He emphasized caring for our brothers and sisters in the faith as our highest priority. Paul confirmed and reinforced this priority when he wrote, "Let us do good to all people, especially to those who belong to the family of believers" (Galatians 6:10).

It's significant that Jesus focused His final instructions to His disciples on this one command and that He said it *four times* that night (twice in John 13:34, and in 15:12, 17).

These were Jesus' final directives to the disciples, as if He were saying to them (and to us), "If you don't do anything else between now and when I return, make sure that you love one another!"

Week Two

Day 2

Friends with Jesus

Today's study might be the most important message in this book. For me, it's also the most difficult to grasp and live.

1. Jesus isn't friends with everyone. Who does Jesus allow to be His friend (see John 15:12–17)?

2. Why did He set this condition for friendship? In other words, how does loving one another ensure His friendship?

3. How literally does Jesus want us to take His teaching to die for each other (1 John 3:16–17; John 15:13)? What are the practical implications for Christ followers who aren't in situations where they might literally give their lives for a fellow believer?

Jesus commanded us to love each other "just as I have loved you" (ESV). How did Jesus love us?

First, He loved us *unconditionally*. That's at the root of the Greek word *agapē,* which John used in all these passages to quote Jesus. Jesus didn't wait for us to do something worthy of His love (we couldn't). Instead He took the initiative and loved us first. His love wasn't "I will love you *if* " or "I'll love you *when*"; it was simply, "*I love you.*" That's the kind of love Jesus commands us to exercise toward fellow believers—particularly those who are suffering around the world.

Second, Jesus also loved us *sacrificially*. He went so far as to instruct us specif- ically to "lay down our lives" for each other (John 15:12–13). He then demonstrated this love only a few hours later by laying down His life for us. John reinforced this point in his epistle to make it unmistakably clear that our priority should be to give our all for the saints in need and, if necessary, even risk our physical lives for their sakes: "This is how we know what love is: Jesus Christ laid down his life for us. And we ought to lay down our lives for our brothers" (1 John 3:16).

This is how we know what love is: Jesus Christ laid down his life for us. And we ought to lay down our lives for our brothers

---

I've received messages from Christians who live in fear for their lives and are reading *Heirloom Love*. It's easy for me, living in the US, to write these things to fellow American Christians. But I feel overwhelmingly unqualified, knowing that some who are reading this are more likely to pay the highest price for friendship with Jesus. Their faith, courage and willingness to die for His name compels me to live to help them.

Sadly, the New Testament mandate to lay down our lives can seem almost irrelevant to many American Christians, because we view Scripture through a lens that is tinted by comfort and security. It's in the New Testament persecution context that we understand the application and critical relevance of 1 John 3:16. As Jesus' friends, we must intentionally reframe our perspective to that of Christ's global body.

Since Jesus said His friends must be willing to die for one another, how much more does He require us to live for one another? There is no limit to the number of opportunities to care for Jesus' persecuted body. As you continue this study, think about ways that you can deny yourself and take up your cross daily by living for fellow Jesus followers, who are suffering and dying for His name.

4. What are a few ways the Lord is calling you to die every day for Him and for others?

5. On a scale of 1 to 10, with 1 meaning "not ready" and 10 meaning "completely ready," how ready are you to be Jesus' friend? Please explain.

Week Two

Day 3

Peter's Priority

Visit *lumenlife.org/myriam* to meet Myriam, a ten-year-old Iraqi Christian who survived the mass killings and kidnapping of young girls by ISIS. She is one of millions forced from their homes to live in refugee camps. An estimated three million people from around the world have listened to Myriam's words of love and faith, which she says she received from the Holy Spirit. Her viewers would probably agree.

* * *

The freedom and prosperity that we enjoy here in the West makes it difficult for us to comprehend heirloom love. We have to work at grasping the mindset and assumptions with which much of the New Testament was written.

The early church was born and grew in a context of persecution. During the first century, the pre-believer considering faith in Jesus Christ had to weigh the likely cost. He or she might face rejection from family and friends, boycotting by customers or clients (if not complete loss of livelihood), loss of home and possessions, wrongful lawsuits and imprisonment, and possible torture and death at the hands of authorities or other hostile parties.

Certainly there were pockets of Christians here and there who experienced peace and security for limited periods. But as a rule, to be a Christian in the first century was to face the troubles that Jesus predicted for us. When we read and interpret New Testament statements without acknowledging this context of danger, hostility and near-universal suffering and loss, we're likely to miss critical aspects of the meaning of the teachings—often the primary meaning.

Peter wrote to a persecuted and suffering people. He mentioned their suffering in every chapter of his first letter. In his greeting, he referred to them as "strangers in the world, scattered"—as refugees—throughout several large regions in Asia Minor (modern Turkey; 1 Peter 1:1). They "had to suffer grief in all kinds of trials" (1:6). And why were they suffering? Often "for doing good" as Jesus' followers (2:20; 3:17). Peter urged them to follow the example of Jesus in suffering (2:21–25; 4:1). And he wrote to them, "Dear friends, do not be surprised at the painful trial you are suffering, as though something strange were happening to you. But rejoice that you participate in the sufferings of Christ, so that you may be overjoyed when his glory is revealed" (4:12–13). And, "Those who suffer according to God's will should commit themselves to their faithful Creator and continue to do good" (4:19). And, "You know that your brothers throughout the world are undergoing the same kind of sufferings. And the God of all grace, who called you to his eternal glory in Christ, after you have suffered a little while, will himself restore you and make you strong, firm and steadfast" (5:9–10).

It's in this persecution context that Peter wrote one of the key passages for this book: "*Above all things* have fervent love *[agapē]* for one another"(4:8, NKJV).

This statement is rooted in the authentic heirloom love we're trying to recover. Love for fellow believers is an ongoing theme throughout Peter's letter; just as he mentioned his readers' suffering in every chapter, so also in every chapter he exhorted them to love each other (see 1:22; 2:17; 3:8; 4:8; 5:14). Peter would never deny the importance of loving unbelievers; after all, he walked with Jesus and watched Him love every type of person He encountered. But once again we see a priority on showing love toward each other within the worldwide body of Christ.

By the phrase "above all things," Peter stressed that the command to love each other stands as the highest priority. I'm sure Peter considered all his teachings to be important, but like Paul (see Colossians 3:14), he didn't hesitate to proclaim a hierarchy among the Bible's teachings. And at the top of the list is—what else?— Jesus' new command. I believe Peter would agree with this paraphrase: "If you remember nothing else I've written, remember and obey this: Love each other." In the context of Peter's letter, this highest of all priorities had to naturally include generous expressions of love toward the practical needs of persecuted and suffering fellow believers.

Peter's priority—*above all else* to love the saints, especially by caring for those in suffering and persecution—rocked my spiritual world. For years I lived with a complacent conception of the Lord's mandates and priorities. First Peter 4:8 was my wakeup call to what He requires of me. The Lord is using this command and its implications to change my misplaced priorities and overcome my selfish, apathetic inclinations. The implications of this command are significant, and I'm still in the early stages of grasping how it affects my worldview and my life purpose and priorities.

Our calling and duty to show unconditional, tangible, unceasing love toward each other—especially toward saints in tribulation—is an intense, twenty-four-seven responsibility.

Finally, Peter commanded that this love toward one another be "fervent." The Greek word Peter used is *ektenēs,* which means that our love should be vigilant, unrelenting, continual, persevering. Our calling and duty to show unconditional, tangible, unceasing love toward each other—especially toward saints in tribulation—is an intense, twenty-four-seven responsibility.

1. Describe what you imagine life was like—including the emotional struggles—for the recipients of Peter's first letter (see 1 Peter 1:1, 6; 2:18–23; 3:13–17; 4:1–2, 12–19; 5:6–10).

2. Since we find 1 Peter 4:8–11 embedded in a context of persecution, we know that one of its key applications is caring for those suffering for our common faith. What are practical ways Christians who are relatively free to live out their faith can obey 1 Peter 4:8–11?

Week Two

Day 4

John Defines Authentic Christianity

1. **You have suffering brothers and sisters around the world who desperately need your practical expressions of love. What are the implications if you open your eyes and heart to them? What are the implications if you close your eyes to them? (See 1 John 2:9–11.)**

Near the end of the first century, when John wrote his epistles, Christianity had been around long enough that false teachers had arisen—those who found ways to use the name of Christ for personal gain. They mixed enough truth to draw would-be Jesus followers astray with enough falsehood to keep the followers from salvation and eternity.

That's why John wrote his first epistle: specifically to dispel false teachings and to help us know whether we've truly been born again to eternal life. "These things I have written to you concerning those who are trying to deceive you. . . . These things I have written to you who believe in the name of the Son of God, so that you may know that you have eternal life" (1 John 2:26; 5:13, NASB).

John's doctrine on how we can know we have eternal life can be summarized in the following verses: "We know that we have passed from death to life, because we love our brothers. Anyone who does not love remains in death. . . . If anyone has material possessions and sees his brother in need but has no pity on him, how can the love of God be in him? Dear children, let us not love with words or tongue but with actions and in truth. This then is how we know that we belong to the truth" (3:14, 17–19).

Almost 40 percent of the verses in John's letter on authentic Christianity (39 out of 105) pertain to obedience to Jesus' new command to love all the saints. In John's terminology, our sacrificial love for fellow believers is like a birthmark that provides visible evidence of our rebirth and validates the authenticity of our faith. This birthmark is our assurance that we've truly passed out of death and into life. It is the same mark Jesus said would reveal to the world that we're His true disciples (see John 13:34–35).

John was so confident in the inseparable nature of *agapē* love and true faith that he boldly said, "This is how we know who the children of God are and who the children of the devil are: Anyone who does not do what is right is not God's child, nor is anyone who does not love their brother and sister" (1 John 3:10, NIV-2011). He implicitly defined hate as the opposite of love, and so hate describes our refusal to share our abundance with needy fellow Christians (see 3:15 in context with 3:17–18). In fact, in verse 15 John went so far as to say that those who hate are murderers.

It may seem extreme by the standards of this world to say that those who withhold life-sustaining assistance from the poor are guilty of hate and murder. But the King does not judge according to the standard of the world. He judges people, not only according to their actions, but also by their intentions and the attitudes of their hearts. For example, a man can be guilty of adultery if he lustfully looks at a woman (Matthew 5:27–28).

John allowed for imperfection in the believer's conduct (see 1 John 1:8–2:2) if the primary characteristics of one's conduct are doing what is right and loving one's brother and sister. During the years when I lived in ignorance of Christian persecution and the New Testament mandate to love, I was still a believer in Jesus. I was saved. My thinking and behavior was characteristically godly and right in many ways. The same is true for many believers in Jesus today; they may still be in the process of learning to walk in truth, or they've lost their first love and need to repent. These shortcomings alone do not make them "children of the devil."

Still, John used stark language to teach and warn us against being deceived in this most important matter. He said in no uncertain terms that those who do not characteristically express *agapē* love toward fellow believers are children of the devil. Saving belief in Jesus is inseparable from obedience to Jesus' new command. The two are so closely interrelated that John referred to them as one command: "This is his command: to believe in the name of his Son, Jesus Christ, and to love one another as he commanded us" (3:23).

Caring for family is simply something that family does.

---

2. Explain how our agapē love for our brothers and sisters in Christ is our confidence that we have been born of God by grace through faith (see Ephesians 2:8–9) and have received eternal life (see 1 John 3:9, 16–18; 5:1).

3. How did reading John's black-and-white statements about who does and doesn't belong to Christ affect you?

If you've fallen short, in any way, of living as God's true child, John has provided the all-important answer: "If we confess our sins, he is faithful and just and will forgive us our sins and purify us from all unrighteousness. . . . My dear children, I write this to you so that you will not sin. But if anybody does sin, we have one who speaks to the Father in our defense—Jesus Christ, the Righteous One. He is the atoning sacrifice for our sins" (1 John 1:9; 2:1–2). To confess means to agree with God.

Talk humbly, honestly with your Father about anything you need to make right before Him. He is faithful and just to grant you His promised forgiveness and purification.

Week Two

Day 5

James Describes True Religion

James's letter is similar to 1 John—both were written to people who were deceived about what constitutes sin and how to know they had eternal life. As you study James, picture the real Christians who were then, and the millions who are now . . .

- Children robbed of their martyred or wrongly imprisoned Christian fathers.
- Wives robbed of their Jesus-loving husbands.
- Local flocks whose pastors have been murdered or kidnapped.
- Poverty-stricken, lacking access to education or good jobs or confiscated homes and property.

1. How did James describe the "wisdom" that justifies selfish ambition (3:14–16)?

2. How did James describe the wisdom that is from God? (3:13, 17–18)?

From the first verse of his letter, James evidenced his mindfulness of his persecuted readership. James addressed the letter "to the twelve tribes scattered among the nations" (1:1)—a clear reference to the dispersion of Jewish Christian refugees who had fled their homes to escape the "great persecution" (see Acts 8:1; 11:19).

Before the end of the letter's first chapter, we come to a well-known passage that begins, "Do not merely listen to the word, and so deceive yourselves. Do what it says" (1:22). Then notice what James taught as the pinnacle of such obedience: "Pure and genuine religion in the sight of God the Father means caring for orphans and widows in their distress and refusing to let the world corrupt you" (1:27, NLT).

James was echoing an often-mentioned litmus test for the faithfulness of God's people in the Old Testament—caring for widows and orphans (see, for example, Isaiah 1:16–17; 58:6–7). The new factor for James's New Testament readership was that many of the "widows and orphans in their distress" were families of martyred Christians. This ultimate test of "pure and genuine religion in the sight of God the Father" boiled down, in many cases, to caring for victims of persecution. What's more, in verse 27 James asserted that caring for the widows and orphans of the martyred saints is as fundamental and essential to genuine Christian faith as keeping ourselves from being corrupted by the world.

This ultimate test of "pure and genuine religion in the sight of God the Father" boiled down, in many cases, to caring for victims of persecution.

James next addressed favoritism toward the rich over the poor. Many of these poor would have become so when they fled persecution and left behind their possessions and livelihoods (2:1–13). He then launched into the nature of genuine faith (as opposed to "faith" in name only): "What good is it, my brothers, if a man claims to have faith but has no deeds? Can such faith save him? Suppose a brother or sister is without clothes and daily food. If one of you says to him, 'Go, I wish you well; keep warm and well fed,' but does nothing about his physical needs, what good is it? In the same way, faith by itself, if it is not accompanied by action, is dead" (2:14–17).

James's argument continues through verse 26, but these opening verses are enough here to make the point: To illustrate genuine faith, James cited the believer who provides clothing and daily food to fellow believers who are so poor they have neither. Whether this condition was due to persecution or some other cause, the fact remains that many believers among James's readers were destitute refugees fleeing from persecution, and he could think of no greater expression of genuine faith than to provide for such needs within the family of faith.

The essence of James's message through most of chapters 1 and 2 is that respecting and caring for desperately needy Christians is the substance and evidence of genuine faith. James boldly stated that we're deceived (1:22, 26)—he even questioned whether we're truly saved (1:26; 2:13–14, 17, 20, 26)—if we don't show mercy to suffering and persecuted Christians by providing for their physical needs (2:13–15). Doesn't this sound amazingly like John's test of genuine faith? Once again we see that the tangible expression of love toward fellow believers is the ultimate evidence of rebirth.

Since starting our journey into heirloom love, my family has financially participated in various relief projects for persecuted believers. Each of these has been special and uniquely rewarding, but one project stands out as perhaps more gratifying than the others. A season of rioting and Christian persecution throughout a large Asian city culminated with the brutal beatings and murders of dozens of pastors and church leaders—some even set afire in front of their families. In the aftermath, we financially helped the suddenly orphaned children and widows of those brave and faithful men. The money went toward relocating these traumatized, desperate families to safety in other cities, prepaying their rent, providing the widows with the training and means to start home-based businesses, and introducing them to new local churches that would care for them. Although I have never met these grieving families, I am deeply thankful for the opportunity to help them. And I joyfully anticipate meeting them in heaven.

Many organizations do great work reaching out to widows and orphans around the world, but very few seem to give proper biblical weight and priority to the families of the martyred saints. Consequently we tend to neglect the widows and orphans of our murdered brothers and sisters. At most we give them no more attention than the rest of the world's needy. This may seem "fair," but it's not biblical.

3. What are some of the reasons Christians today might be so de-
    ceived as to neglect their suffering brothers and sisters?

    James 3:14

    James 4:4

    James 5:1–5

Week Two

Day 6

Real Life in Eritrea

Worship from a Metal Box

Picture a scene of rocky desert on the southern outskirts of Africa's Sahara. No vegetation, not even a scrub bush in sight. Clouds are rare, the sun beats down on every square inch and daytime temperatures commonly top 90 degrees F, sometimes climbing to a searing 100 and higher.

Now put a metal shipping container in the middle of this flat, desolate landscape—a truck-sized steel box like one that might be loaded onto a train or a ship. Its battered, oxidized surface absorbs the sun's rays and creates an ovenlike environment inside. This container sits sealed shut, out in the desert heat day after day after day.

Next imagine eighteen or twenty emaciated men or women crammed into this metal container, confined continuously for weeks and months and years, their bodies baking all day long, gasping for breaths of fresh air through one paperback-book sized hole in the wall.

Finally, picture dozens of such shipping containers arrayed across the parched landscape, "housing" hundreds of suffering people. This is Mai Serwa prison camp outside Asmara, Eritrea.

This is also a site of sacred worship. The rusty containers comprise a cathedral of sorts, housing among the inmates an unknown number of Jesus followers and seekers, a flock of spiritual sheep. Their number is strong and growing, in large part because just a few years ago their shepherd was a frail thirty-year-old woman named Helen Berhane.

Helen always loved her country—a small, war-torn nation on the east coast of Africa. Its population is nearly half Muslim and nearly half Orthodox Christian. The government allows practice of these and the Catholic and Lutheran faiths, but evangelical Christianity was outlawed in 2002. The paranoid government suspects evangelical Christians to be spies against the state; thus these brothers and sisters are granted no freedom to congregate, worship or even possess a Bible.

Eritrea is known as the "North Korea of Africa" for its brutal treatment of its own citizens. Twenty thousand people are currently imprisoned there without charge or trial. These include, at any one time, an estimated 10 percent of Eritrea's evangelical Christians; 50 percent of the nation's Christians have been imprisoned at some time during their lives. Why? Because their consciences prompt them to worship according to a tradition differing from those allowed by the government.

It was in this hostile context that the Lord called Helen to serve as a shepherd caring for His sheep. Ever since her childhood she knew she was meant to serve the Lord with her life, and in her late twenties she found herself leading and teaching a flock of hungry followers.

And she sang. Oh, how she sang! The Holy Spirit gifted Helen to inspire others through her songwriting and singing. In fact, she published an album of worship songs that proved popular among Eritreans; it was distributed widely through the underground churches.

Then one night, as our sister was teaching in a secret church meeting, she was arrested in a raid. Helen's punishment for the crime of worshipping in an unauthorized church was thirty-one straight months of imprisonment, most of it in her shipping container home in the desert. When Helen arrived at Mai Serwa prison camp, she discovered that inmates were kept sealed in their containers most of the time. Once or twice per day she was allowed to use the "toilet"—a flat, open area of rocky ground a half-mile from camp. Otherwise she had to use a bucket in one corner of her container. Men and women were segregated into separate containers, though one of the most frightening punishments for a female inmate was to be forced to sleep among the male prisoners; rape and a resulting pregnancy would almost certainly kill the woman in the camp's harsh conditions. Inmates were shuffled around and sometimes crammed together with more bodies than space permits to sleep at one time on the uneven floor. So they would sleep in shifts, rotating to preferred locations, away from the stagnant puddles from dripping condensation and farthest from the stench from the toilet bucket.

Helen's diet varied unpredictably and was never adequate for sustaining health. Sometimes the food was purposefully made inedible, by over-salting, for example. Medics were available merely to keep prisoners alive, not to keep them healthy.

Guards regularly punished inmates for making noise, for looking out of the breathing hole, or just because a guard was having a bad day. Christian prisoners received the worst treatment in the camp. Every time new prisoners arrived, a Christian—often Helen herself—was brought out and tortured as an example intended to frighten the new prisoners into submission.

Throughout her imprisonment, officials used beatings, exposure to the extreme heat and cold, and other forms of torture to pressure her to recant her faith. Repeatedly she was offered freedom; she need only sign a document promising forever to discontinue her ministry activities. Repeatedly she refused. Instead, Helen persisted in singing praises, teaching the Bible, praying with others and smuggling Scripture-based messages of truth and encouragement. She was caught and punished many times, and at each turn this simple-hearted, steadfast sister courageously declared her intention to continue obeying her Lord.

Helen had once read Richard Wurmbrand's *Tortured for Christ,* in which the author wrote of his experience in prison: "We could not be prevented from singing, although we were beaten for this. I imagine that nightingales, too, would sing, even if they knew that after finishing they would be killed for it." Helen found it impossible *not* to sing.

Helen sang of the brave heroes of the Bible, who looked forward to a better country.[8]

At the same time she loved her earthly country, Eritrea, whose government punished her for her loyalty.

Helen sang about peace and joy from the Lord—both so valuable that no earthly loss could compare.

Her torturers could only shake their heads in bewilderment.

Helen sang about hope and salvation, even for her tormentors.

---

[8] Hebrews 11:13–16: "All these people were still living by faith when they died. They did not receive the things promised; they only saw them and welcomed them from a distance, admitting that they were foreigners and strangers on earth. People who say such things show that they are looking for a country of their own. If they had been thinking of the country they had left, they would have had opportunity to return. Instead, they were longing for a better country—a heavenly one. Therefore God is not ashamed to be called their God, for he has prepared a city for them."

Her jailers shouted all the louder to drown out her message—but some were listening, learning.

Helen sang about love and forgiveness. She loved and prayed for her guards and even felt sorry for them; in some ways this was as much a prison for them as it was for her. Spies were recruited to trap Helen with evidence of her persistent "wrongdoing." Instead, she won them over with love and the Lord's truth; they would not betray her.

A few of the guards secretly joined Helen's flock, learning about Jesus and God's Word. Helen continued to write Bible lessons for prisoners throughout the camp—Christians and not-yet-Christians alike—smuggling them around and receiving smuggled messages in return. Her ministry helped rescue many from eternal darkness, from suicide, from depression, from the traps of hatred and bitterness.

The reputations of Helen and other Christians became well known throughout Mai Serwa, and former skeptics began to wonder about this Jesus for whom someone would endure so much.

Finally, after catching Helen smuggling a Bible message, officials became so exasperated that one of the camp chiefs—a Muslim named Suleiman, well known for his methodical torture—called Helen before him. She wasn't chained; everyone at Mai Serwa knew Christians didn't fight back.

Suleiman trembled with rage. A police baton lay at hand. Helen trembled with terror in spite of her faith. Suleiman raised the baton to strike.

Helen raised her eyes to Jesus, the Lamb who remained silent even when beaten.[9]

Suleiman systematically beat Helen over every inch of her body.

By her Lord's grace, Helen endured in silence. Not a cry, not a whimper.

"Leave us alone, Helen!" Suleiman began to scream, in rhythm with his fearsome blows.

Helen's existence was nothing but agony and Jesus.

Suleiman became so fatigued he had to rest. Then he resumed.

When he'd finished, Suleiman had Helen dragged back and chained in the searing sun outside her container. She knew she was dying; she would soon see Jesus.

---

[9] See Isaiah 53:7.

Camp medics discovered Helen's condition; one of them, seeing her head-to-toe wounds, had to leave the examination room to cry.

Over the next several days the medics, fearful of a death on their watch, implored Suleiman to send Helen to the Asmara hospital. Suleiman refused; he was trying to cover up his actions.

Helen deteriorated, losing blood, unable to stand, eventually unable to urinate. Her breathing was restricted by swelling in her neck. She lay for days in her container, praying for Suleiman's repentance and salvation and continuing, as she was able, to write Bible lessons and messages of encouragement for her flock. The mistreatment continued—even another beating. Throughout her endless torment, the Lord's nightingale sang.

Then came the day Suleiman relented, and Helen was released. She had been in prison for thirty-one months and two weeks.

With proper medical treatment and the attentive care of her family, Helen slowly recovered in the hospital. But she was not out of danger. In light of the near-certainty that she would be reincarcerated as soon as she was well, Helen escaped from her beloved country, miraculously, to neighboring Sudan, where her sister cared for her.

Helen soon learned that she was not yet beyond the clutches of the Eritrean authorities. She moved to secret locations several times, but each time she began to receive anonymous threatening phone calls.

She applied to several nations for asylum and finally found security and freedom in a new home, Denmark.

Helen has shared her story in a book titled *Song of the Nightingale*. She still loves her home country and longs for a day when the powers of darkness there no longer crush the sons of light. Perhaps that day will come by way of the collective voices of Western Christians and other freedom lovers.

To this day Helen continues her ministry wherever and however the Lord leads her.

She has never stopped singing.[10]

---

[10] Sources: Helen Berhane, *Song of the Nightingale* (London: Authentic Media, 2009); "CSW Month of Campaigning for Eritrea Culminates in Launch of Gospel Album," Christian Solidarity Worldwide, June 2, 2006, csw.org.uk/2006/06/02/press/517/article.htm; "Eritrean Gospel Singer Helen Berhane Released from Prison," Christian Solidarity Worldwide, November 3, 2006, csw.org.uk/2006/11/03/press/569/article.htm; now-unavailable report, Assist News, accessed April 23, 2013, assistnews.net/stories/2013/s13040060.htm.

Week Two Group Discussion Guide

After completing Days 1–5 and reading the real life story, meet with your group and use this discussion guide to help you "spur one another on toward love and good deeds" (Hebrews 10:24).

PRAY (10 minutes)

Invite one or two volunteers to share persecution news stories they've read during the week. Pray for your spiritual family in these stories.

Ask the Lord also to help you know His love for you, and to fill you with love for Him and for others. Consider basing your prayer on Ephesians 5:1–2; 8–10:

Follow God's example, therefore, as dearly loved children and walk in the way of love, just as Christ loved us and gave himself up for us as a fragrant offering and sacrifice to God. . . . For you were once darkness, but now you are light in the Lord. Live as children of light (for the fruit of the light consists in all good- ness, righteousness and truth) and find out what pleases the Lord. (NIV-2011)

SHARE (40 minutes)

Share with the group your thoughts and discoveries from the following questions:

Day 2, question 4 and 5

Day 3, question 2

Day 4, questions 2 and 3

Day 5, questions 2 and 3

Share your thoughts about real life in Eritrea.

CLOSE (10 minutes)

Pray for the Christians in Eritrea. Ask the Lord to:

- Save Eritrea's president and the other governmental leaders.
- Turn the Eritrean authorities' hearts to allow God's people to worship Him peacefully.
- Strengthen and grow His church in Eritrea.
- Keep the Eritrean Christians' faith from failing.
- Release the Christian prisoners who are being held in the desert prison camps.

Pray for yourselves, that the Lord's Word will transform you, helping you see and love people the way He does.

Ask for one or two volunteers who will each take a few minutes during the upcoming week to read the latest persecution news and briefly share one or two news stories at your next meeting. Persecution news is available at *LumenLife.org/ news*.

WEEK THREE

Love Lived

"If we love our brothers and sisters who are believers, it proves that we have passed from death to life."

—John, 1 John 3:14 (NLT)

Day 1   Loving Him Is Loving Them

Day 2   Legendary Love

Day 3   Acceptable Worship

Day 4   Paul's Proof Point

Day 5   Kingdom Heart, Kingdom Mind

Day 6   Real Life in Burma: Languishing Within Reach of Rescue

Group Discussion Guide

Loving Them Is Loving Him

Week Three

Day 1

Loving Them Is Loving Him

Use the following link to watch a one-minute introduction to *Heirloom Love* Week Three:

LumenLife.org/hlvideos

1. Paul was on his way to persecute Christians when Jesus appeared to him on the road to Damascus. Why did Jesus say that Paul was persecuting Him, when it was other people Paul was going after (see Acts 9:1–5)?

2. How does Jesus view our efforts to care for His needy brothers and sisters (see Matthew 25:34–40)?

3. How does Jesus view us when we reject or neglect His needy brothers and sisters (see Matthew 25:41–46)?

It should be enough that Jesus commanded us to love each other. But we tend to subconsciously filter the Lord's commands, paying attention to certain ones while neglecting others. Sadly, I did this for years with Jesus' new command. But through my difficult experiences I'm learning how critical it is that we *agapē* love each other.

To help us appreciate the importance of His new command, Jesus explained that our *agapē* love for the saints is inextricably linked with our love for Him: "If you love me, you will obey what I command. . . . This is my command: Love each other" (John 14:15; 15:17). The implication in context is that we express love for Jesus by obeying His new command, loving each other.

Concrete, practical, in-the-flesh love for fellow believers is the same as love for Jesus Himself. This is what Jesus was saying in Matthew 25:34–40, when He said that those who care for "the least of these brothers of mine" are ministering directly to Jesus the King. When we minister in any way to persecuted and suffering saints, we are really ministering to the Lord Jesus Christ.

When we minister in any way to persecuted and suffering saints, we are really ministering to the Lord Jesus Christ.

Conversely, when opponents persecute Christians, they are really persecuting Jesus. When the apostle Paul (then named Saul) was stopped by a dazzling light and a booming voice on the road to Damascus, he was in the middle of a systematic campaign to hunt down, imprison and if necessary execute the followers of Jesus. But when he asked the obviously supernatural being, "Who are you, Lord?" the voice answered, "I am Jesus, whom you are persecuting" (Acts 9:5).

Jesus says to us, His followers, "He who rejects you rejects me" (Luke 10:16). And many years after his conversion, Paul would write, "When you sin against your brothers . . . you sin against Christ" (1 Corinthians 8:12).

But sin against Jesus need not be only through persecution of His followers—a sin of *commission,* actively doing what is wrong. We also sin against Jesus by our sin of *omission* when we passively fail to do what is right. When we stand before our Lord and Judge, it won't be enough to stammer, "But I didn't hurt anyone." He will require an accounting of whether we acted upon the many opportunities He has given us to do good. Jesus made it clear that forgetting or neglecting the needs of "the least of these" is equivalent to rejecting Him.

> Then he will say to those on his left, "Depart from me, you who are cursed, into the eternal fire prepared for the devil and his angels. For I was hungry and you gave me nothing to eat, I was thirsty and you gave me nothing to drink, I was a stranger [refugee] and you did not invite me in, I needed clothes and you did not clothe me, I was sick and in prison [unjustly] and you did not look after me."
>
> They also will answer, "Lord, when did we see you hungry or thirsty . . . ?"
>
> He will reply, "I tell you the truth, whatever you did not do for one of the least of these [brothers and sisters of mine], you did not do for me."
> (Matthew 25:41–45)

For many years I neglected these Scriptures and was ignorant of this calling. I thank the Lord for His gentle rebuke and for removing the scales from my eyes. One day I look forward to seeing His smile and hearing Him say, "You cared for My brothers and sisters; you cared for Me."

4. **How can you become more consistently mindful that loving Jesus requires caring for the least of His people? And that failing to care for the least of His people is failing to love Jesus?**

Week Three

Day 2

Legendary Love

1. Read about what life was like for faithful Christians in Hebrews 10:32–34. In your own words, describe the cost of faithfulness for those who were imprisoned and for those who helped the imprisoned.

2. How did the Hebrew Christians benefit from helping their imprisoned fellow Christians? Write your own paraphrase of Hebrews 6:10, using Malachi 3:16–18 to help you understand it.

3. How did the Hebrew Christians' unity and love for one another most likely impact the watching world around them (see John 13:34–35; 17:20–23)?

The writer to the Hebrews affirmed a full equivalency between the readers' physical ministry to the Lord's people and directly loving the Lord Himself: "God is not unjust; he will not forget your work and the love you have shown him as you have helped his people and continue to help them" (Hebrews 6:10).

We further understand the writer's meaning when we grasp that he was writing during a time of severe persecution. He was extolling his readers for loving the Lord, specifically through their ministry to persecuted Christians. Believers lived in fear for their lives, and many of them stopped meeting together because it was dangerous to be seen associating with other Christians (10:25). Those who ministered to persecuted believers showed their love for the Lord and His children by risking their lives to help them.

Those who ministered to persecuted believers showed their love for the Lord and His children by risking their lives to help them.

"You endured a great conflict of sufferings, partly by being made a public spectacle through reproaches and tribulations, and partly by becoming sharers with those who were so treated. For you showed sympathy to the prisoners and accepted joyfully the seizure of your property, knowing that you have for yourselves a better possession and a lasting one" (10:32–34, NASB). Christians who were caught helping their suffering brothers and sisters had their homes and property confiscated. Many believers were imprisoned during this time, and first-century prisons did not provide prisoners with life-sustaining necessities. These imprisoned believers were dependent on Christians on the outside to bring them food, water, clothing, and medical care—and their brothers didn't let them down. The early church members loved Jesus and one another so much that they knowingly incriminated themselves by publicly visiting the imprisoned saints to provide for their bodily needs.

The writer to the Hebrews referred again to his readers' dire straits in his closing remarks: "Let love of the brethren continue. Do not neglect to show hospitality to strangers, for by this some have entertained angels without knowing it. Remember the prisoners, as though in prison with them, and those who are ill-treated, since you yourselves also are in the body" (13:1–3, NASB).

When reading this, remember the thousands of Christian refugees described in Acts 8:1, and multiply the picture many times over in the following decades, before this letter was written. A massive number of Jesus' followers who weren't imprisoned were forced on short notice to leave behind homes, possessions, livelihoods and friends. Early believers everywhere were commanded to risk everything to care for these homeless and imprisoned brothers and sisters. Obedience to Jesus' new command was perilous work that separated Jesus' true friends from the hypocrites.

The Hebrew Christians loved one another "just as" Christ loved them. This is heirloom love, the legendary Christian love that changed the world.

4. **In Week Two, Day 2, on a 1–10 scale you rated your readiness to be Jesus' friend. Now imagine what being Jesus' friend would mean if you were a free first-century Hebrew Christian (or a twenty-first-century Christian in many places). At risk of your freedom and maybe your life, friendship with Jesus would mean publicly walking to the prison to bring food, clothing and medical care for fellow Christians. In this scenario, are you just as ready as in Week Two to be Jesus' friend? Is your rating (on a 1–10 scale) the same as before, or does it change? Please explain.**

Week Three

Day 3

Acceptable Worship

Paul and the Jerusalem church leaders understood that the Lord had called Paul to take the gospel to the gentiles (Galatians 2:7–9; Acts 26:12–18). But they also agreed that he should care for poor Christians, which Paul said was "the very thing I was eager to do" (Galatians 2:10).

1. Why would Paul accept the added burden of raising funds for the poor, when it might distract him from his main calling? Did he misunderstand God's assignment to him? Or did the two tasks somehow belong together as part of one mission? How?

2. How do you define worship?

3. Paul taught Romans 12:8, 10, 13 as forms of worship that are acceptable to the Lord (12:1). Hebrews 13:1–3 also presents forms of "acceptable worship" (12:28–29). Read these passages and explain how they clarify your understanding of worship that the Lord values and accepts.

What is worship? According to the Bible, our worship must include more than what we do in our church services if it is to be pleasing and acceptable to the Lord. And, as we're about to see, caring for suffering Christians is one of the most pleasant and fragrant forms of worship.

We've seen that the writer to the Hebrews gave us a strong exhortation to "show hospitality to strangers" and to "remember those in prison . . . and those who are mistreated" (Hebrews 13:2–3). If we look back just a couple of verses from there, we see that these specific actions are biblical expressions of acceptable worship (Hebrews 12:28). The author was telling us to worship the Lord with reverence and awe—by caring for persecuted and suffering saints.

Caring for suffering Christians is one of the most pleasant and fragrant forms of worship.

The apostle Paul was passionate about supporting suffering and persecuted believers, and his passion was rooted in his understanding of worship. Consider his instruction in Romans 12:1: "I urge you, brethren, by the mercies of God, to present your bodies a living and holy sacrifice, acceptable to God, which is your spiritual service of worship" (NASB). Apparently not all worship is acceptable to the Lord. Notice the verses following Romans 12:1, where Paul provided examples of acceptable worship: "Contributing to the needs of others . . . give generously. . . . Be devoted to one another in brotherly love. . . . Share with God's people who are in need. Practice hospitality" (12:8, 10, 13).

According to Paul, contributing to the needs of the saints is an acceptable sacrifice of worship. What's more, Paul's very example underscored the global nature of this responsibility. He wrote the letter to the Romans, from which we just read, while carrying a generous relief gift from the believers in Macedonia and Achaia (in modern Greece) to the suffering Christians in Judea (see Romans 15:25–26). This was a thousand-mile journey that required months and many perils. The barriers between the European believers and their Judean brothers and sisters were far greater in their day than the barriers between us and anyone else in our world. But these Christians worshipped in a significant and tangible way by reaching out to fellow believers in need.

The Macedonian believers exemplified acceptable, fragrant worship. They were suffering their own financial hardships, yet they were more than willing to help suffering believers in Jesus. Paul boasted about their amazing worship: "Out of the most severe trial, their overflowing joy and their extreme poverty welled up in rich generosity. For I testify that they gave as much as they were able, and even beyond their ability. Entirely on their own, they urgently pleaded with us for the privilege of sharing in this service to the saints" (2 Corinthians 8:2–4).

THE PRIVILEGE OF SHARING

The churches Paul planted demonstrated a supernatural unity and sacrificial love for one another—even when the givers themselves were suffering persecution. This begs the question: What was Paul teaching his converts to cause them to give "even beyond their ability" to help suffering Christians in a foreign land—people they would never meet in their lifetimes?

We discover some of Paul's foundational convictions in the letter he wrote to churches in Galatia (in modern Turkey). Here Paul reported an important visit he paid to the church leaders in Jerusalem: "James, Peter and John, those reputed to be pillars, gave me and Barnabas the right hand of fellowship when they recognized the grace given to me. They agreed that we should go to the Gentiles, and they to the Jews. All they asked was that we should continue to remember the poor, the very thing I was eager to do" (Galatians 2:9–10).

Paul's calling was to carry the light of the gospel to the Gentiles. However, his ministry was also defined by his passionate and persistent advocacy and fundraising for the poor, suffering and persecuted believers. Peter, James and John—back at Jerusalem Central—were so emphatic that ministry to the suffering saints should be a priority that they conditioned their blessing of Paul's mission on his fulfilling of this responsibility, alongside his evangelism. But the needs of his suffering brothers and sisters were already heavy on Paul's heart.

Later in this same letter, Paul clarified the believer's obligation to care for all people. But he also made it unmistakably clear that the highest priority was to care for fellow Christians (Galatians 6:10). Paul taught and supported this priority throughout his ministry.

In Paul's first letter to the believers at Corinth (in Achaia), we see that he was collecting money on behalf of suffering and persecuted saints: "Now concerning the collection for the saints, as I have given orders to the churches of Galatia, so you must do also: On the first day of the week let each one of you lay something aside, storing up as he may prosper, that there be no collections when I come" (1 Corinthians 16:1–2, NKJV). This is the only reference to Sunday offerings in the New Testament; the purpose of these offerings was explicitly for the benefit of suffering believers in a foreign land.

By the time Paul wrote his second letter to the Corinthians, his advocacy for the persecuted had proven so successful that he could say, "The ministry of this service is . . . *fully* supplying the needs of the saints" in Judea (2 Corinthians 9:12, NASB). These were more than mere token offerings; they were substantial gifts for the relief of thousands of Christians. God accepted their worship, and He was glorified.

Week Three

Day 4

Paul's Proof Point

Second Corinthians 8–9 presents the most comprehensive teaching in the Bible of Christian giving. But we often overlook its original context, so let's take a fresh look.

1. Read 2 Corinthians 8:1-5, in which Paul said the extremely poor Macedonians gave "beyond their ability." What do you imagine they gave up in order to help other Christians?

2. What motivated the Macedonians to "beg" (NASB) or "urgently plead" (NIV) to help suffering Christians in a foreign land (8:4)? (Consider also 2 Corinthians 5:14-16.)

3. Have you ever begged for an opportunity to give? How and why are you like or unlike the Macedonians?

4. Based on 2 Corinthians 8:13–15, describe God's economy and His reasons for giving only some people an abundance.

5. What makes financial giving an indicator or "proof" of our love (see 2 Corinthians 8:24)?

Second Corinthians 8–9 is full of biblical principles about giving that you may have read or heard taught many times. As we examine this discourse, keep in mind that Paul issued these teachings in a specific context—to raise financial support for Christians in a faraway land who were suffering, probably due to persecution.

Paul started this discourse with a case study on the Macedonian Christians (in northern Greece). The Macedonians were more than just poor, they were destitute. But they had Jesus' joy, in keeping with Jesus' promise in John 15:10–12, and they gladly sacrificed from their insufficient supply of life-sustaining necessities. They even begged for a chance to help other suffering Christians (8:1–5).

They were begging out of deep gratitude for "the grace of our Lord Jesus Christ, that though he was rich, yet for your sake he became poor, so that you through his poverty might become rich" (8:9). Their giving was motivated by Christ's love and grace, not by legalism or coercion. This reminds me of my recent experience. As I write this, hundreds of thousands of Nigerian Christians, including countless children, are starving to death because they've been driven from their homes and farms by Islamists. Last month I was praying about how much to give for their food relief, and the Lord said to me, *Dominic, that's Me in Nigeria. I'm hungry and I'm watching and waiting to see who loves Me and will give Me something to eat* (see Matthew 25:31–46). I began weeping as I thought about His love and all that He has done for me. I and would have begged, if necessary, for a chance to feed my hungry brothers and sisters.

Paul, like Jesus, Peter, James, and John, taught that helping suffering Christians should be a high priority for us. Paul commended the Corinthian believers (in southern Greece) for several areas of their obedience. Then, to put in perspective their need to provide for the suffering saints, he said: "Just as you excel in everything—in faith, in speech, in knowledge, in complete earnestness and in your love for us—*see that you also excel in this grace of giving*"(2 Corinthians 8:7).

Pause and consider what Paul was saying: Helping suffering Christians is just as important a priority as faith, prophecy and knowledge.

Paul explained that we *prove* our confession of the gospel and our love for one another by generously supporting the suffering saints: "Openly before the churches, show them the proof of your love and of our reason for boasting about you" (8:24, NASB). Words come easily. "We love God and we love people," say millions of Christians. But where's the proof? How can others tell that these claims are true? Paul said we prove it by caring for suffering brothers and sisters around the world.

We love God and we love people," say millions of Christians. But where's the proof?

Paul is also our source for the "law of the harvest": "Whoever sows sparingly will also reap sparingly, and whoever sows generously will also reap generously" (9:6). This teaching has a variety of valid applications, but we miss Paul's central meaning if we forget that he was referring to helping suffering Christians. We could paraphrase it, "The Lord will sparingly reward those who sparingly support their suffering brothers and sisters; and the Lord will generously reward those who generously give to the needs of suffering believers in Christ." Take a moment to consider this amazing promise as it was originally intended. God will generously reward the one who shares with suffering fellow believers in Jesus. Are you ready to trust God and test His promise?

Many of us fear we won't have enough to help others while also caring for our own families. Some of the generous Macedonians—who went hungry in love for those even more impoverished—probably struggled with the decision. We can imagine mothers and fathers talking quietly at home: "If we make sure the children have food every day, I don't mind missing a few meals for a while. And we can make our clothes last another year." They were confident in the Almighty, who owns all wealth in the universe, whose resources are limitless. Just as Paul reminded the Corinthians:

> God is able to make all grace abound to you, so that in all things at all times, having all that you need, you will abound in every good work. As it is written: 'He has scattered abroad his gifts to the poor; his righteousness endures forever.'

> Now he who supplies seed to the sower and bread for food will also supply and increase your store of seed and will enlarge the harvest of your righteousness. You will be made rich in every way so that you can be generous on every occasion, and through us your generosity will result in thanksgiving to God. (9:8–11)

Building on his mention of thanksgiving to God, Paul explained that our love for suffering saints brings worship and glory to the Lord: "This service that you perform is not only supplying the needs of God's people but is also overflowing in many expressions of thanks to God. Because of the service by which you have proved yourselves, men will praise God for the obedience that accompanies your confession of the gospel of Christ, and for your generosity in sharing with them and with everyone else" (9:12–13).

Note Paul's wording: The Corinthians didn't just speak words (their "confession of the gospel"), but by accompanying their confession with "obedience" and "generosity in sharing," they "proved" their words genuine. Our support for the suffering saints should be a natural and inextricable outflow of our confession of the gospel. It's unnatural to profess Christ while not caring for persecuted coconfessors.

Light will overcome the darkness as we show the proof of our confession and our love. Lives will be changed. Our brothers and sisters in other parts of the world will praise and thank God, "and in their prayers for you their hearts will go out to you, because of the surpassing grace God has given you" (9:14).

And, of course, the apostle finished as we should start and finish, by praising the Source of it all: "Thanks be to God for his indescribable gift!" (9:15).

Amen.

Week Three

Day 5

Kingdom Heart, Kingdom Mind

1. How do wealth, possessions and worldly pursuits affect our heart toward the Lord and His kingdom? (See Matthew 6:19–34; Luke 8:14–15.)

2. Based on Revelation 3:14–22, write three to five sentences characterizing the Laodicean Christians.

3. Translate Revelation 3:18 into practical advice for Christians like the Laodiceans who want to repent.

4. Describe the privilege and relationship that Jesus gives to those who repent (see 3:19–21)?

5. How can we, who have material goods in abundance, gain from the eternal wealth of God's faithful among the poor (see James 2:5; also Matthew 5:3)?

When we shape our hearts and minds around God's kingdom, we come to understand clearly His will for the abundance He gives some of us, His children. God wants us to share our abundance, and He condemns selfish consumption and hoarding, even if it's motivated by worry for our own provision (Matthew 6:19–34; Luke 12:15–34; 16:19–31; James 5:1–5).

When I started on this journey to heirloom love, I only understood the persecuted church's need for us. I didn't realize how much we need them. Our need for them is confirmed in James's reminder: "Has not God chosen those who are poor in the eyes of the world to be rich in faith and to inherit the kingdom he promised those who love him?" (James 2:5; see also Matthew 5:3).

God has entrusted His suffering children with an abundance of faith, hope, perseverance, zeal and kingdom-mindedness. We need more of these Jesus-like character qualities in American Christianity. I didn't realize that I was spiritually blind, poor and lukewarm until I embraced our persecuted family. To my shame I was a poster child for the Laodicean church's attitude (see Revelation 3:14–22).

The Laodicean church truly believed they were walking in the light, but Jesus said they were lukewarm (3:15–16). They were deluded and spiritually blinded by their abundance. That's why Jesus said, "You do not know that you are wretched and miserable and poor and blind and naked" (3:17, NASB).

Sometimes you need to know what hot is before you can truly see lukewarm for what it is. I didn't realize how lukewarm I had become until I visited some Christian brothers in a foreign country who were serving the Lord amid life-threatening persecution. These brothers take up their crosses and literally risk their lives daily in order to share the gospel, make disciples and help persecuted brothers and sisters. I spent the day with a courageous brother who, several weeks prior, had been attacked by men with machine guns and left for dead, because he had been preaching the gospel. The Lord miraculously healed him, and he was still proclaiming the gospel in that same area when I arrived. I was more than a little nervous hanging out with him that day.

Sometimes you need to know what hot is before you can truly see lukewarm for what it is.

I was privileged to visit this brother's home and share a meal with his family. I saw that they accept these difficulties as normal life for those who love Jesus and obey the gospel. Just a few months after my visit several men clubbed to death another brother from that church in front of his family, and another was shot in the back of his head and killed in his driveway—because they were Christians.

When I returned home from this trip, I was reading Jesus' message to the church in Laodicea, and the Lord convicted me that I was lukewarm. My experience with my persecuted spiritual family had made obvious what it means to be "hot" for Jesus—and that "hot" wasn't me. I was the weak link, possibly even a hindrance to the truly faithful. In hindsight my hope and prayer should have been that my misguided, self-preserving, lukewarm, creature-comfort-oriented interpretation of Christianity didn't cause my zealous brothers and sisters to stumble.

Jesus' appeal came from grace and love. He didn't just point out the Laodiceans' (and our) faults, but for their and our benefit He graciously counseled the pursuit of pure "gold" (eternal wealth), "white clothes" (His righteousness) and "salve" for our spiritual eyes (for healing and true sight). And He assured that His rebuke and discipline are expressions of His love (3:18–19).

He ended His rebuke: "Here I am! I stand at the door and knock. If anyone hears my voice and opens the door, I will come in and eat with him, and he with me" (Revelation 3:20). This passage is often misunderstood. It's not Jesus calling the lost to salvation, but Jesus calling believers to repent from hoarding and excessively consuming the world's goods, which blind and chill our hearts toward Him. In fact, He invites us, not only into intimate fellowship, but also to reign with Him on high (see 3:21)!

Among those who will reign with Christ are several Jesus followers of Potiskum, Nigeria. Last year a suicide bomber detonated a bomb during the morning service at Redeemed Christian Church in. Tabita Adamu and two of her children died in the bombing. Four of Tabita's children survived because, shortly before the bomb blast, she sent them home to get money for the offering. After the attack Tabita's brother Habila said, "We know that going to church is a matter of life or death. But we have already in our mind that no one can stop us from worshipping our God, no matter the risks. We thank God because he always gives us the ability to stand for Him."

Habila speaks from experience. The Islamic group Boko Haram invaded his home three years ago. While Habila's wife and young son watched, the invaders held an AK-47 to his head and asked if he was a Christian or Muslim.

He said, "I am a Christian."

They said he could live if he would say, "There is no god but Allah, and Muhammad is his messenger."

Habila replied, "I am a Christian and will always remain a Christian, even to death."

Visit *LumenLife.org/Habila* to hear what happened next. In this amazing story we can learn something about the gospel and following Jesus, something we might not otherwise learn in our insulated American lives.

6. **How is your spiritual temperature?**

Week Three

Day 6

Real Life in Burma

Languishing Within Reach of Rescue

What do you see? Statistics or stories?

A quarter million Burmese refugees are languishing in India, Thailand and China, living in circumstances little better than those they fled. That's a statistic.

But a story begins like this: "Thirty-year-old Biathleng fled [Burma][11] for Delhi in June, with three children and a teenage wife." This is the first sentence of a New York Times report—our only snapshot of the day-to-day existence of these five individuals. Their five true stories are representative of the millions of individual, first-person stories that get lost in the statistics.

Let's consider the story of a young man, his teenage wife and their three little ones—a story that the five of them haven't simply read or heard about; they've lived every excruciating second.

This young Christian family left behind their homes and everything they knew. Why? Because Burma is now heavily militarized, ruled ruthlessly by the hostile Buddhist majority who have been persecuting Christians for more than five decades. Biathleng left behind discrimination and forced labor, false accusations and arbitrary detentions. He and his family fled summary executions and

---

[11] Although the official name of this Southeast Asian country is now Myanmar, we'll use the older, familiar and still commonly used name, Burma.

conscription of children off the streets for combat. They ran from rape and extortion and burning of homes and churches. Biathleng and his wife and children went in search of freedom to practice their faith, on a quest for authorities who might lend a just and sympathetic ear.

They went also in search of food, fleeing the unrelenting famine of their homeland. Burma's government offered no relief to the country's predominantly Christian minority and refused to allow humanitarian aid to the region where Biathleng's family lived.

Biathleng's family realized they weren't going to survive in their homeland, so they decided to cross into neighboring India. They gathered what they could carry and spent two days crossing the ten thousand-foot-high Arakan Yoma mountain range. That brought them to India's isolated Mizoram state, which is comprised of about 90 percent Christians.

Sounds ideal, doesn't it? Christian refugees among Christian hosts. A God-given opportunity for the family of Jesus to care for its own.

Not so. The reputation of the Lord and His church is soiled.

On the whole, the refugees are unwanted and unloved. Picture Biathleng—a father desperate to protect and provide for his young family—required to compete with Indian nationals for inadequate food, medical resources and jobs. More than once, Mizoram has sponsored movements to push the Christian refugees back across the border. The central Indian government refuses even to recognize the refugees' existence, let alone provide humanitarian treatment for those who have fled for their lives.

What about international relief? The United Nations High Council on Refugees (UNHCR) exists for the purpose of helping people like Biathleng find their way to survival resources and eventually to resettlement in a welcoming host country. Where is the UNHCR in India? Not in Mizoram state. In fact, the Indian government allows the relief organization to operate in only one city—Delhi, in the heart of the Indian subcontinent. In recent years more than ten thousand Burmese have traveled to Delhi in search of official recognition of their refugee status and the meager benefits that come with it.

In pursuit of their refugee cards, Biathleng and his family shared a vehicle going north from Mizoram state for three hundred miles, then managed train fare for the additional thousand miles west to Delhi.

Imagine bringing your tiny, impoverished family of five to Delhi, the fourth-most-populous city in the world, with more than twenty-two million people and a population density of thirty thousand per square mile. Imagine not knowing the language and searching its labyrinthine quarters for housing and other basics of survival. Biathleng found a home for his wife and three young children, together with four other "roommates." The nine of them still live in this single eight-by-twelve concrete room, part of a mazelike tenement building. Fifteen rooms—housing approximately one hundred men, women and children—share a single toilet. Drinkable water is scarce, so the family suffers chronic illnesses—jaundice, diarrhea and dysentery—and rarely leaves their tiny home. When they're able, they attend Sunday worship meetings and their oldest boy attends a small nongovernment school where he learns English and Hindi—languages essential for survival in Delhi. Otherwise they huddle in their concrete box day and night, hour after long hour; they cannot tolerate the city's pollution except when absolutely necessary, and someone must protect their few possessions from theft.

At the time of Biathleng's story, he was waiting for an appointment for his UNHCR refugee card. Because of limited access to the UNHCR and the organization's inefficiency, Biathleng can expect the process from beginning to end to require twelve to eighteen months. Some cases take years, and some people literally die waiting. Even if Biathleng and his family survive the wait, rejection is a real possibility. In the years that the UNHCR has been operating in Delhi, only a few thousand Burmese refugees have been approved, and only a few hundred new approvals are processed each year—not nearly enough to keep up with the thousands of new refugees arriving annually in Delhi.

The benefits of approval? Well, they don't include up-front financial support; India phased that out in 2011. The refugee card is not a work permit; that requires a separate application. The credentials don't protect their owners from rampant resentment and discrimination by their Indian neighbors. Legal protection? Police pay little heed when detainees produce their refugee cards.

So what do people wait a year or more to acquire? A limited medical reimbursement is available, payable several months after the medical expense is incurred. And some qualified refugees find third-country placement, mainly in Canada, the US, Australia and Europe.

Meanwhile the refugees pine away like prisoners, by the thousands, in the dust, heat, smog and cultural isolation of Delhi.

Religious and ethnic discrimination and abuse affect all the refugees. They arrive unable to speak Hindi or English, with no clear avenues for learning. When they're able to find work, they're underpaid, if paid at all. The government has set the poverty line at the equivalent of a little over two American dollars per day; many Burmese work twelve-hour days for close to half of that. Instantly recognizable as foreign, the Christians from Burma are subject to frequent harassment, assault and rape. Picture Biathleng, frantic to glean anything edible for his wife and children, taking the risk of scouring market sites at night for discarded or rotten vegetables, competing with locals and animals for the scraps.

Our brothers and sisters in Christ have been abused, starved and driven from their homeland in Burma. Our spiritual siblings have worked hard and traveled far in search of basic life necessities and the freedom to live for Jesus. And still they suffer.

Christians who have fled Burma to other countries are no better off. They flee east into Thailand, where, by recent figures, 140,000 Burmese refugees stagnate in isolated mountain camps. They flee north into China, where refugees have recently been deported by the thousands back to Burma—back into the thick of armed conflict and religious persecution—contrary to China's own law and violating international laws signed by China.

Think of all the unbelievers out there who have read the New York Times article about Biathleng's plight. They have good reason to scoff at Christianity, in light of the inactivity and apparent disinterest of Christ's global family. For the sake of our witness before the watching world, we must help. We must seek updated reporting about persecution in Burma, which is readily available online. We must pray fervently for our brothers and sisters in Burma and in equally horrendous circumstances as homeless refugees in neighboring countries. We must make our voices heard through the channels of power and influence, pressing Burma, India, Thailand and China to treat our family with dignity and care. And where secure avenues become available, we must share our wealth so that Biathleng and his little tribe might enjoy one or two healthy meals per day.

As it is, millions of Christian refugees suffer in the "havens" to which they've fled, hoping for our biblical hospitality. The world scoffs at the apparently uncaring Western church. The Lord weeps.

And for Biathleng, his wife, his three little children, this existence—every second, every minute, every hour, every day—is neither a story nor statistic. For them, it's life.[12]

---

[12] Sources: Rajni George, "Life in Limbo for Chin Refugees," *New York Time,* November 30, 2011, india.blogs.nytimes.com/2011/11/30/life-in-limbo-for-chin-refugees; Michelle A. Vu, "Illegal Aliens or Refugees? 100,000 Burmese Chin Christians in India," *Christian Post*, March 6, 2012, christianpost.com/news/illegal-aliens-or-refugees-100000-burmese-chin-christians-in-india-70954/#TYjdApjlTetwBRMr.99; Trent Franks, "Franks Statement on Human Rights in Burma" (speech presented in Tom Lantos Human Rights Commission hearing February 28, 2013), US Congressman Trent Franks's official website, franks.house.gov/franks-statement-human-rights-burma; Brendan Giusti, "Burma Christian Persecution: At Least 10 Killed in Grenade Attack on Orphanage," *Christian Post*, November 14, 2011, christianpost.com/news/burma-christian-persecution-at-least-10-killedin-grenade-attack-on-orphange-61673.

Week Three Group Discussion Guide

After completing Days 1–5 and reading the real life story, meet with your group. We offer this guide for your discussion.

PRAY (10 minutes)

Start by sharing members' newly read persecution news stories. Then pray for your spiritual family in those true stories. Ask the Lord to burden your hearts with His concerns and to open your minds to His truth. Pray for each other's growth in submission to Him and for a deeper love relationship with Him.

SHARE (40 minutes)

Share with the group your thoughts and discoveries from the following questions:

Day 1, questions 2 and 4

Day 2, question 4

Day 3, question 3

Day 4, questions 3 and 5

Day 5, questions 1, 3 and 5

Share your thoughts about real life for Burmese Christians.

CLOSE (10 minutes)

- Pray for the hundreds of thousands of Burmese Christians who've had to flee their homeland and need hospitality.
- Pray for yourselves, for hearts and minds devoted fully to God's kingdom, and for His great joy as your reward.

Ask for one or two volunteers to read the latest persecution news and briefly share stories at your next meeting. Persecution news is available at *LumenLife.org/ news.*

WEEK FOUR

Love Tested

"I am not commanding you, but I want to test the sincerity of your love."
—Paul to the Corinthian church, 2 Corinthians 8:8

Week Four

Day 1

Love Without Hypocrisy

Use the following link to watch a one-minute introduction to Week Four of your journey to heirloom love:

LumenLife.org/hlvideos

* * *

God has commanded us to love and do good to all people, especially to the family of believers (see Galatians 6:10). Given the immense worldwide need, we need to ask, How much should I give? And, What is a legitimate standard of living for my family and me? The more modestly we live, the more we have available to help others.

These are difficult questions, to which I know no simple answers. And the answers for you are probably different from mine. Even within my own family we don't always agree. I have erred on both sides—on the side of frugality to a fault and, at other times, on the side of overspending and excessive consumption. Although I don't have all the answers, I can share the truths the Lord has used to guide me on the journey into heirloom love.

The Lord has provided us with a key principle to help guide our decisions about how much we keep and how much we give. It's not a way of measuring our giving, but a God-given way of measuring our hearts and our love. It's called sincerity.

We've seen that Paul urged a lifestyle of worship, acceptable to God (see Romans 12:1). In spelling out the details of such a life, Paul taught, "Love must be sincere. . . . Be devoted to one another in brotherly love. . . . Share with God's people who are in need" (12:9–10, 13). One true expression of worship is *sincere love*, expressed through sharing with Christian brothers and sisters in need. The Greek word Paul used for "sincere" is *anupokritos*. It's created by connecting the prefix *an-* (meaning "not" or "without") with the word *hupokritēs,* from which we derive our word "hypocrite." In fact, the NASB translates it "without hypocrisy." In ancient Greek culture, a *hupokritēs* was an actor who wore a mask on stage to represent his character. So hypocrisy is putting on an act, wearing a mask or disguise, presenting a front to hide what is underneath. And its opposite (not-hypocrisy) is open, undisguised sincerity.

A God-given way of measuring our hearts and our love. It's called sincerity.

Therefore, Paul taught that one guideline for the expression of sincere love is that it has nothing to hide. When "love" is hiding something, it holds back and does less than it is able. Paul said that "the gift is acceptable according to what one has" (2 Corinthians 8:12). Our sincerity—and the Lord's acceptance of our offering—is measured in part by our ability. If we claim to love and it's within our means to help, yet we choose to do less than we could—due to indifference or selfishness— we're hypocrites. We're hiding something.

Of the many words Jesus used to describe people, perhaps one of the most condemning was "hypocrite" (see, for example, Matthew 6:2, 5, 16; 23:13–39). He clearly defined a hypocrite when He described the Pharisees' pattern of teaching one thing and living another: "You must obey them and do everything they tell you. But do not do what they do, for they do not practice what they preach" (23:3). Jesus was much more patient toward sinners who honestly admitted their failures (for example, Matthew 9:9–13). He would not tolerate hypocrites—those who hid their wickedness under a mask of righteousness. He challenged all of us to "come clean"—to stop hiding so He can cleanse us and fill us with sincere love.

The first disciples to be called Christians (at Antioch, see Acts 11:26) demonstrated love without hypocrisy by giving as fully as they were able: "The disciples, each according to his ability, decided to provide help for the brothers living in Judea" (11:29).

Paul presented the Macedonian church as a model for sincere obedience to Jesus' new command (see 2 Corinthians 8–9). These fellow believers also passed the sincerity test—they were without hypocrisy and had nothing to hide. They so loved their needy, faraway brothers and sisters that they gave "even beyond their ability" (8:3).

1. Scripture relates our giving to our "ability." But one of the things hypocrisy hides is our *true* ability. Describe your fullest giving ability in terms of the ways you use your:

   a. Time (which you could use to learn about and pray for the persecuted).

   b. Relationships (through which you could spread awareness of the persecuted).

   c. Money and possessions (which could be used to care for the persecuted).

   d. Freedoms and skills (which can be used to advocate for and help the persecuted).

2. Describe how hypocritical "love" (masked, hiding) can influence your giving and everyday lifestyle.

3. Hypocrisy also hides from our *responsibility*. Scripture says, "You are not your own; you were bought at a price" (1 Corinthians 6:19–20), and everything within our *ability* belongs to the Lord, to be used for His purposes. What, if any, changes is the Lord leading you to consider in order to sincerely love your imperiled brothers and sisters?

Week Four

Day 2

Love That Is Pure

1. What did Paul mean when praying that our love would increase "in real knowledge and all discernment" (Philippians 1:9, NASB)? (Consider also James 3:13–18.)

2. Why did Paul say it's important for our love to grow in this way (see Philippians 1:10)?

Paul's prayers give us insight into some of his highest priorities and concerns for the church. The following prayer for the Christians at Philippi (one of the Macedonian cities) is especially pertinent to our topic: "This I pray, that your love *[agapē]* may abound still more and more in real knowledge and all discernment, so that you may approve the things that are excellent, in order to be sincere and blameless until the day of Christ" (Philippians 1:9–10, NASB).

Here in the NASB we find again the word "sincere," this time translated from Paul's choice of the Greek word *eilikrinēs*. This word is a compound of *heilios* ("sun") and *krinos* ("judge, test"). It literally means "judged by sunlight" and relates to certain trades in the ancient world. For example, when a maker or buyer of pottery or fabric wanted to discern a product's quality, one way was to hold it up and allow sunlight to shine through it. This would reveal any defects in a weave or hairline cracks in baked clay. The word came to apply to anything that was somehow tested and demonstrated to be free of defects or impurities—for example, gold or silver that contained no alloys.

When our knowledge and discernment of truth become sullied with the world's thinking, we begin to approve and follow the world's misguided values.

For us to pass this test of purity or "sincerity," Paul prayed that we might "abound still more and more in real knowledge and all discernment, so that you may approve the things that are excellent." When our knowledge and discernment of truth become sullied with the world's thinking, we begin to approve and follow the world's misguided values. When we adopt even a small degree of materialistic thinking, we start to lose our ability to discern the Lord's will and begin investing our resources in things of temporal value, rather than people and causes with eternal value. Truth becomes warped, our vision becomes darkened and blurred by the world's influence. And our love becomes misguided, so that it no longer passes the sincerity test for defects. Our consumption-driven Western culture has distorted the terms "ability," "need" and "disposable income." Most of the world's population—the portion that doesn't share in our freedom and material abundance—is more likely to be "sincere" or pure in their thinking about these terms.

Consider the following true story of a pastor whose ministry I work with. The pastor, from a third-world country, was visiting the US for the first time. Many people in his country are slowly perishing due to a lack of food, medical care and other life-sustaining resources. The average life expectancy for an adult male in his country is only forty-seven years (compared to seventy-five in the US). Many of his people often go one or more days without food, and when they do eat, they typically have only one meal a day, which consists of one scoop of beans and one scoop of rice.

This pastor openly wept when he saw that we have animal hospitals, while many of his people are perishing for lack of basic medical care. He cried out to the

Lord and asked if he and his people were less than human because the Lord gave animal hospitals to the Americans but has withheld even the basics for life from his people.

This pastor has the real knowledge and discernment to help us see through our religious veneer, our self-justification and our cultural desensitization. He can objectively identify our blind spots, the impurities in our vision, the cracks in our love. He knows the difference between worldly "love" and sincere love. I wonder how he would counsel us if we invited him into our homes and allowed him to review our finances and our schedules. Would I truly listen? Would you?

IN SEARCH OF SINCERE LOVE

The sincerity of our love is the measure that guides what we give and what we keep. None of us begins with perfectly sincere love; we grow and transform over time, as we conform to the likeness of the Lord Jesus Christ. Along the way we wrestle with individual choices: Is the Lord honored if we replace our car or buy a boat or update our clothes? For some of us in some situations, He is. For others, such spending would be an unloving decision. Every decision must be guided by the question: Is this an expression of biblically sincere love, as described in the Scriptures we've just studied?

When in doubt, sincere love errs on the side of generosity. And when we "lose" something for the sake of love, the Lord has a way of replacing our loss with something even greater (see Mark 10:28–30).

Two thousand years ago a person was considered prosperous and able to help others if he or she owned a second coat or had a second loaf of bread (see Luke 3:11). The standard for determining ability may have changed since then, but the Lord still requires that we express sincere love by living modestly and sharing our abundance. Those who sincerely love the children of God will temper their consumption in order to give as much as possible from their time, money and other resources to help persecuted and suffering fellow believers.

We need to grow in knowledge and discernment about how to manage our abundance in view of the global needs of the body of Christ and the poor in general. I admit that for many years I did not contribute to the needs of persecuted Christians. At the time I lived in half ignorance, half denial. I was preoccupied and comfortable with my life and the treasure of this world that makes a man lukewarm toward the kingdom of God and His children. By the Lord's grace I have since repented and the Lord is fanning into flames my otherwise shamefully lukewarm heart. As a result I'm learning to temper my consumption and live modestly so I can contribute more to my brothers and sisters in tribulation—that my love might be sincere: pure and without hypocrisy.

3. It can be hard to separate out worldly pollution from godly thinking. Consider the "wisdom" that guides your daily decisions. List a few principles that you can say with confidence are biblically wise, that are certain to produce unpolluted, sincere love.

4. Now list a few principles of the world's "wisdom" that are incompatible with pure, sincere love.

5. How might you apply this sincerity test to a decision you're facing now—some use of your time, talent, treasure, relationships and more? Which of your possible choices best reflects love that is pure and true, rather than polluted?

Week Four

Day 3

Straining Gnats, Swallowing Camels

I've tried to make a biblical case for the following thesis: How much we help the least of the saints, according to our ability, is a litmus test that indicates how much we love them, and therefore how much we love the Lord. It's up to you to study the Scriptures and decide whether this is true.

While on your journey, you may need to examine your doctrine on giving and ask whether it's supported by Scripture. Many American Christians today believe our financial obligation to the Lord and the body of Christ is a tithe (10 percent) of our income to our local church. After that, according to this school of thinking, we are free in God's eyes to spend the other 90 percent any way we wish.

But tithing is not authorized in the New Testament. A more detailed consideration of tithing is presented in my book *Prodigal's Progress: From Loving Money to Loving God.* But the bottom line is, while the New Testament is filled with early church teaching and examples of giving, Christian giving is never associated with a percentage. Nowhere in the New Testament does the Lord say that Christians should give 10 percent of their income. Nor are there any examples or inferences in Scripture to lead us to believe the early Christian church might have taught or practiced tithing.

While the New Testament is filled with early church teaching and examples of giving, Christian giving is never associated with a percentage.

The command to tithe originated in the Old Testament Mosaic law. At that time the Lord commanded His people to give an offering of two tithes (a total of 20 percent) every year and a third tithe (for a total of 30 percent) every third year.[13] In Acts 15:1–30, the Lord released us from tithing when the apostles said we need not observe the law of Moses except "to abstain from food sacrificed to idols, from blood, from the meat of strangled animals and from sexual immorality" (15:29).

Some people say that Jesus condoned tithing for Christians in Luke 11:42: "Woe to you Pharisees, because you give God a tenth of your mint, rue and all other kinds of garden herbs, but you neglect justice and the love of God. You should have practiced the latter without leaving the former undone." Consider also the parallel passage (Matthew 23:23–24), where Jesus continued, "You blind guides! You strain out a gnat but swallow a camel." Jesus wasn't teaching that Christians should tithe. Rather, He was rebuking the Jewish leaders, who were supposed to be living according to the Mosaic law. If Jesus had intended this passage to apply to Christians, we should be giving 20 percent every year and 30 percent every third year. However, the context and teaching in this passage is not about tithing but about the common human temptation and tendency to love money more than people. It's about our tendency to delude ourselves and deceive others by using religious traditions to mask our greed and self-indulgence.

Jesus' new command requires that we sacrificially share our abundance with our suffering brothers and sisters. This command cannot be reconciled with any teaching that limits our love obligation to some degree below our ability. We cannot sincerely love one another while limiting our assistance to a percentage or any other standard that condones indulgence or hoarding while others suffer and die.

* * *

Following are four Scripture passages we've already studied. Read each one carefully. Keep in mind the original context and intended meaning when Jesus, Paul and John spoke or wrote these words. Imagine also the faces of our brothers and sisters whose stories you've been reading throughout this book.

A new command I give you: Love one another. As I have loved you, so you must love one another. (John 13:34)

My command is this: Love each other as I have loved you. Greater love has no one than this, that he lay down his life for his friends. You are my friends if you do what I command. (John 15:12–14)

---

[13] See Leviticus 27:30, 32; Numbers 18:24, 28; Deuteronomy 12:11–12; 14:28–29.

I urge you, brothers, in view of God's mercy, to offer your bodies as living sacrifices, holy and pleasing to God—this is your spiritual act of worship. (Romans 12:1)

This is how we know what love is: Jesus Christ laid down his life for us. And we ought to lay down our lives for our brothers. If anyone has material possessions and sees his brother in need but has no pity on him, how can the love of God be in him? Dear children, let us not love with words or tongue but with actions and in truth. (1 John 3:16–18)

1. **In the light of the preceding passages and everything you've read in this book, how much of your time, talent and treasure does the test of sincere love allow you to consume or keep for yourself?**

2. **Pray for yourself and your group, asking to be filled and driven by the love described in these passages. If you gain new insights or convictions, write them below.**

Week Four

Day 4

That the World May Believe

"No one has ever seen God; but if we love one another, God lives in us and his love is made complete in us." (1 John 4:12)

Wouldn't it be wonderful if any honest unbeliever could observe the Christian community and conclude that Jesus is the only Savior, sent from God? Imagine if by our conduct these dear, lost people could see enough of God in us to cause them to trust us and listen to our message.

A dream, you say? Impossible? Well, it's Jesus' Plan A, and He didn't allow us the option of any Plan B. Furthermore, He made it our responsibility to bring it to reality. How? By obeying His command to love one another.

We've spent most of this book exploring Jesus' new command: to love one another in the same way Jesus has loved us (John 13:34). Now let me remind you of Jesus' next sentence: "By this all men will know that you are my disciples, if you love one another" (13:35). On the night before His impending crucifixion, Jesus was concerned about our witness before the watching world. And His plan for convincing the world was the unmistakable testimony of *agapē* love within the church, *from* all of His followers *to* all of His followers.

Later that evening, Jesus prayed. He prayed for us. He revealed His plan and how it would be fulfilled:

"I pray . . . that all of them may be one, Father, just as you are in me and I am in you. May they also be in us *so that the world may believe* that you have sent me. I have given them the glory that you gave me, that they may be one as we are one: I in them and you in me. May they be brought to complete unity *to let the world know* that you sent me and have loved them even as you have loved me." (John 17:20–23)

The Lord's plan and design is that the world will see Him—His goodness and glory—through us as we model sacrificial brotherly love and unity in the body of Christ. Jesus said that our unity and *agapē* love for one another is our "glory"—given to us by the Lord (17:22). And the witness of this glory would cause the world to "believe" and "know" the saving truth about Him.

BOUND BY LOVE

"Jesus gives the world the right to judge whether you and I are born-again Christians on the basis of our observable love toward all Christians."

—Francis Schaeffer

How often do we remember that our evangelistic success depends on *agapē* love flowing like blood throughout Christ's body? And how well do we understand that the body we must love is worldwide? Our sacrificial love is the bonding agent that unites the body of Christ and is therefore an essential prerequisite to successful evangelism. "And over all these virtues put on love *[agapē]*, which binds them all together in perfect unity" (Colossians 3:14).

Our sacrificial love is the bonding agent that unites the body of Christ and is therefore an essential prerequisite to successful evangelism.

The early church modeled unity by their *agapē* love for one another, even to the point of selling their possessions to provide life sustaining necessities for their poor brothers and sisters. They demonstrated pure and undefiled religion (see James 1:27), which powerfully validated Jesus as Lord and the authenticity of His disciples. This validation fueled rapid church growth in Jerusalem despite the high risk of persecution for those who decided to follow Jesus Christ. People were literally dying to follow Jesus—so strong was the early church's witness of love.

The apostle Paul's successful ministry is our biblical model for apologetics, evangelism, church planting and making disciples. It's no mere coincidence that Paul was also a passionate advocate and fundraiser for the persecuted saints. His ministry modeled the unity and *agapē* love that Jesus said would cause the world to know and believe that He was sent from heaven. Paul's tangible love for the suffering church was foundational to his evangelistic success.

In American Christianity today we have impressive ministry plans and budgets for international justice, disaster relief, humanitarian aid and economic development for impoverished non-Christians in distant parts of the world. These efforts are all good, all part of the Lord's purpose for His people.

But unlike Paul, we have developed an international reputation for not caring for our own—the Lord's suffering children. I spoke to an American Christian leader who attends conferences on persecution. He meets church leaders from persecuted countries, and they frequently ask him why American Christians are aloof and indifferent toward their suffering brothers and sisters.

How can non-Christians believe that Jesus is the Son of God, that we are His disciples, and that we love everyone, when it appears that we don't love the Lord's suffering children—our family? How can the world believe that we love the Lord, whom we have not seen, if it appears we do not love our brothers and sisters whom we have seen (see 1 John 4:20)? As we saw in the earlier story about forgotten Burmese refugees, as publicized by the *New York Times*, our hypocrisy obscures the beauty and excellence of Christ's body and hinders the world from knowing and believing that Jesus Christ is Lord.

Fifty years ago, Martin Luther King prophetically warned us, "If today's church does not recapture the sacrificial spirit of the early church, it will lose its authenticity, forfeit the loyalty of millions, and be dismissed as an irrelevant social club with no meaning for the twentieth century." The good news is that it's not too late. We can still demonstrate the sacrificial love that will cause our light to shine before people in such a way that they will glorify our Father who is in heaven (see Matthew 5:16).

* * *

Carefully read these descriptions of heirloom love in the first-century church:

All the believers were together and had everything in common. Selling their possessions and goods, they gave to anyone as he had need. Every day they continued to meet together in the temple courts. They broke bread in their homes and ate together with glad and sincere hearts, praising God and *enjoying the favor of all the people.* And the Lord added to their number daily those who were being saved. (Acts 2:44–47)

All the believers used to meet together in Solomon's Colonnade. No one else dared join them, *even though they were highly regarded by the people.* Nevertheless, more and more men and women believed in the Lord and were added to their number. (Acts 5:12–14)

1. Note the connection in Acts between the believers' love for each other and their growing numbers. What is it about sincere love within the body of Christ that makes Jesus attractive to those outside?

2. How "highly regarded" are American Christians today? How much do we enjoy "the favor of all the people"?

3. How might your answers to the last question be explained by our obedience (or not) to Jesus' new command: "Love one another as I have loved you"? How might it relate to our tangible love for believers in most desperate need—the persecuted?

Week Four

Day 5

Will We Prove Faithful?

1. Paraphrase Galatians 5:13 in your own words.

2. What are some of the more common ways that American Christians tend to use their freedom, comfort and security?

3. We must manage faithfully these valuable blessings from God (see 1 Corinthians 4:2). What are some practical ways that we can become more faithful stewards of our freedom, comfort and security to obey Galatians 5:13?

In 1995, Michael Horowitz, senior fellow of the Hudson Institute, published an op-ed article about Christian persecution in the *Wall Street Journal.* This was during the first of two holocausts in Sudan (the second is ongoing today), in which genocidal dictator Omar al-Bashir slaughtered millions of Christians among his own people. In his article Horowitz wrote that the American Christian community's "moral authority will be gravely tarnished if it fails to exercise its growing political influence on behalf of people now risking everything to engage in the simple act of Christian worship and witness."[14] In other words, our witness will be worthless, and our moral message will be thrown out and trampled underfoot by men, if we do not turn from our hypocrisy and remember our brothers and sisters who endure prison and affliction.

Mr. Horowitz has been proven right. We've lost much of our moral authority and influence since his editorial was written twenty years ago. Are we willing to acknowledge that our sin of silence, while millions of our brothers and sisters have been murdered and inhumanely treated, has contributed to the darkness that is overtaking America?

Our forefathers suffered and risked their lives so we could have religious freedom today. We're stewards of this liberty, and "it is required of stewards that they be found faithful" (1 Corinthians 4:2, ESV). If we fail to use our God-given, constitutional freedom of religion to obey the imperative of Jesus' new command, what hope do we have for the success of our evangelistic efforts? And what hope do we have that the Lord will hear our prayers and allow us to continue in this rapidly fading liberty? "You, my brothers and sisters, were called to be free. But do not use your freedom to indulge the flesh; rather, serve one another humbly in love" (Galatians 5:13, NIV-2011).

The context of this passage in Galatians is freedom from the law of Moses—a freedom belonging to every Christian. However, the principle also applies to economic and religious freedom, which is *not* the privilege of every Jesus follower, but currently entrusted to only the relative few. Our freedom and prosperity is a trust from the Lord that must be used for serving one another, locally and globally, to build up of the body of Christ.

Ravi Zacharias succinctly summarized the consequences of our indifference toward our persecuted brothers: "The silence of the many on behalf of the some will only breed evil that ultimately destroys us all."[15] Zacharias is not suggesting

---

[14] Quoted in Dr. Dobson's April 1997 newsletter.

[15] Ravi Zacharias wrote these words in his afterword to Nina Shea, *In the Lion's Den* (Nashville: Broadman Holman, 1997).

that self-preservation is the primary motive in ministering to the persecuted saints; he's reminding and warning us, as Paul did: "Do not be deceived: God cannot be mocked. A man reaps what he sows" (Galatians 6:7).

Ravi Zacharias: "The silence of the many on behalf of the some will only breed evil that ultimately destroys us all."

In his book *The Future of Christians in the Middle East*, Dr. Habib Malik validates Zacharias's prediction. Dr. Malik is a Lebanese Christian with a Harvard doctorate in intellectual history, and he's a professor of history and cultural studies at Lebanese American University. He writes that Western indifference to the fate of Arab and other Middle Eastern Christians has contributed to their decline and peril. He also points out that our blindness has imperiled the West and that the defense of religious freedom for persecuted Christians in the Middle East is both a moral and strategic imperative.

The unsaved world is looking and longing for the perfect love that comes from above, which apart from Christ is nothing more than a hollow echo in the souls of men. What they see within the global body of Christ will not only influence their future, but perhaps ours as well. For the sake of their eternal salvation and for our continued enjoyment of liberty, we must express biblical love for God's persecuted children around the world.

4. What, if any, changes do you think the Lord is leading you to make in response to what you've learned in Day 5?

Week Four

Day 6

Real Life in India

OUT-CASTES FOR CHRIST[16]

Ten-year-old Namrata knows she's running for her life. The Hindus have already begun attacking homes in the village. They're literally out for blood—Christian blood.

Namrata scrambles and stumbles to keep up with her two sisters. Her eighteen-year-old sister, Trusita, is leading them through the night to the home where she works as a maid when she isn't in school. Maybe they'll be safe with the Das family—also a Christian household, but better off and less likely to be attacked than Namrata's family, a family of agricultural day laborers. A family of Dalits.

Dalits. The lowest of India's supposedly outlawed caste system. Dalits like Namrata are still treated as they're often called: "untouchable."

The Christians in Namrata's village have heard rumors of a wave of violence overtaking Orissa state in recent days. Three days prior, a well-known Hindu leader was assassinated. A Marxist group has taken responsibility for the killing, but this inconvenient fact isn't preventing Hindus from stirring up Orissa's Hindu majority, convincing them that Christians were behind the assassination and are trying to take over the country.

---

[16] Some aspects of Namrata's perceptions of events are fictionalized, but she and the events portrayed are completely real.

In a sense, the Hindus' fears aren't totally unfounded. Faith in Jesus Christ has been gaining a strong foothold in Orissa, India's poorest state. Orissa once reported only 2 percent Christian population. But since people have started coming to Christ by the thousands—especially among the Dalits and minority tribal peoples—even the Hindu nationalists have acknowledged that Orissa's Christian population has reached more than one in four. They're fearful of what would happen to India's Hindu purity and domination if Christians belonging to the lower castes were ever to exercise their full voting power. Intimidation and physical assaults are the Hindus' only hope for forcing these masses to return to Hinduism.

So when Namrata's parents received warning earlier this evening that the Hindus had begun attacking Christians and burning homes here in their village, they were ready to take action. After sending their children off to the Das household, they fled to the nearby forest to join other Christians to wait out the attack.

The three girls arrive at the Das home safely and are welcomed by the family. But soon their fears come true; they hear angry shouts approaching, then pounding on the door. Even this home won't escape the murdering marauders. The host family, along with Namrata and her sisters, hurry to hide in a small bathroom. The pounding on the door becomes more insistent, until they hear the door broken in and angry men entering, violating the sanctity of the home. Loud profanities. Smashing furniture, shattering crockery. Every crash, every shout makes Namrata jump. Each time a new wave of cold washes over her from head to toe. *Make it stop!* she wants to scream.

Then . . . *smoke!* The house is being set on fire!

Namrata wants to run. It's so hard to hold still. But she knows escape is not yet possible. If anyone gives away their hiding place . . .

She has heard the stories, and throughout each long, terrifying minute her racing mind with its vivid imagination can't help replaying each horror in graphic detail. Stories of rape, torture, brutal murder. Stories of people doused with kerosene and burned alive.

The smoke seeping into the bathroom adds to her growing dread. Unthinkably horrific, to burn alive. Will it happen to her tonight? What else might the maddened invaders do to her if they find her?

In the darkness Namrata and her sisters cling to one another.

And Namrata clings to Jesus. Only He can bring them through this safely.

Dear Jesus, she prays, *please don't let the men find us. Please protect us from the fire.* She trembles in terror.

The noises gradually give way to silence. The cowering believers wait to be sure the attackers have actually gone. Slowly they open the bathroom door. Smoke billows in; they hear the crackling of flames, but no evidence of the attackers.

They stealthily emerge to a scene of roiling devastation. Flames lap and flicker here and there. Across the floors are strewn all the household's possessions, mostly in unrecoverable pieces.

They venture to the broken front door and open it a smallest fraction. In the distance they hear angry shouts, frightened screams, crashes and crackling flames. But the attackers have moved on; they're unlikely to come back.

While the others timidly make their way outside, ever watchful for danger, Namrata finds herself strangely fascinated by the ruin that surrounds her. She surveys the scene. Every dish lies in broken bits. Here a smoldering bed, there a pile of burning books. She walks past a dresser that is surprisingly intact.

Deafening blast! Instant inferno. Her body is thrust across the room, crashing against the opposite wall. All goes dark . . .

* * *

Namrata comes back to consciousness days later in a hospital eighty miles from her home. Her whole body hurts—especially her face. And what is all this white goo on her face? She touches it and starts to smile. But it hurts to smile. Why?

Her mother—overjoyed to see her daughter awake—explains. The attackers, before they left the house, planted a bomb in the dresser. It detonated just as Namrata was standing next to it. The explosion severely burned her face and left shrapnel wounds on her face, hands and back—over 40 percent of her body.

The day after the attack, her parents returned from the forest. When they first saw the Das home in charred ruins, they feared all had died in the flames. What joy to find that all were alive! Only to turn back to anxiety when they discovered the still-unconscious Namrata. They anxiously tended her on the long journey down from the mountains to the hospital at the coastal city of Brahmapur.

Namrata doesn't leave the hospital until mid-October, a month and a half later. Her recovery is long and her face will be disfigured the rest of her life. What thoughts and emotions does she grapple with during the long months of her healing? Trauma and fear. Embarrassment and shame at the permanent marring of her once-pretty face. Anxiety about her health and her future.

And anger. Who wouldn't wrestle with anger—even hatred—toward those who attempted to kill her entire family, who took away everything they owned, who damaged her body so horribly, whose continued threats still prevent them from returning to live among their friends and family?

The humble Dalit family spends a short time in an Orissa refugee camp before being relocated with the help of a Christian relief organization to the huge city of Bangalore, eight hundred miles away from their mountain village. Will they ever return? Or are they destined to live as wanderers, robbed of stability and security?

Perhaps Namrata strives mightily with these and other questions and emotions—a battle no ten-year-old should have to face. But in the end she rises the victor, for the autumn months prove to be a period of both physical and emotional healing. By the time she speaks with a news agency in December, she has achieved a settled peace that few mature adults reach, even after several decades of life experience.

Heed the words of a child: "We forgive the Hindu radicals who attacked us, who burned our homes." Namrata's attitude is nothing short of a miraculous demonstration of the Lord's Holy Spirit living inside her. She's grateful to be alive, trusting herself to the Lord's care. Her deepest desire is that her attackers might discover the amazing love of Jesus, come to salvation and spend eternity worshipping in heaven beside her.

Namrata loves Jesus. And Namrata loves her enemies. If she could, she would take them by the hand and lead them to Him.

In more than a dozen of India's twenty-eight states, violent persecution of Christians has been on the rise over the last many years. Christians by the hundreds are being murdered for their love of Jesus. Thousands more are beaten, tortured, raped and falsely arrested. Thousands of homes and churches have been burned.

The perpetrators are almost always Hindus. The police usually turn a blind eye to these activities, and sometimes it's even the "law enforcement" authorities themselves who step in as the brutal aggressors.

More than fifty thousand Orissa Christians fled their homes during the months of death and fear in which Namrata was caught up. Many lived for years in the forest or under tarps in refugee camps. Several years after the violence, many thousands remain homeless.

Those are large, impressive numbers. Now look past the numbers to the mass of personal pain and loss they represent. The cumulative grief, the collective sorrow. The terror and agony of those attacked, the suffering of those bereaved. The persistent confusion and uncertainty for those who have lost everything. The years of toil to regain some semblance of a normal life.

Meanwhile, Indian Christians like Namrata wish nothing but good toward their nation and their persecutors.

Namrata's face and body will never be the same. But while the outer Namrata might be wasting away, the inner Namrata is glowing brighter and brighter day by day.

"They were out of their minds," she explains, believing the best about her attackers. "They do not know the love of Jesus. For this reason, I now want to study so that when I am older I can tell everyone how much Jesus loves us." You see, Namrata has a plan for her life—a plan she believes comes from her Lord: She wants to spend the rest of her days sharing God's message. "This is my future."

Jesus is her inspiration. Pain is her strength. Love is her theme.

The future won't be easy for Namrata or her family. The lowly Dalit family possesses virtually nothing in material terms. But they all maintain joyous hope because of the eternal spiritual wealth they possess in Jesus Christ—a wealth they gladly share.

"The world has seen my face destroyed by the fire," Namrata says, referring to the picture of her scarred visage that has been posted across the Internet. "Now it must come to know my smile full of love and peace."

Beauty. Submission. Obedience. Forgiveness. Relentless love. These are the qualities that grow and blossom within a girl with the maturity to match her appearance—that of a wizened older woman. It's fitting that Namrata's family name, "Nayak," means "hero." Let us allow Namrata's example to inspire us to follow in her tiny bare footsteps.[17]

---

[17] Sources: Nirmala Carvalho, "Orissa: Christmas of Namrata, the Little Dalit Disfigured by a Bomb," AsiaNews.it, December 15, 2008, asianews.it/index.php?l=en&art=14009&size=A; Teresa Neumann, "Christian Girl, Disfigured by Bomb, Forgives Terrorists," Breaking Christian News, December 20, 2008, breakingchristiannews.com/articles/display_art.html?ID=6162; "Será Possível Esquecer?" Voz da Verdade (Voice of Truth), November 4, 2012, vozdaverdade.org/site/index.php?id=2918&cont_=ver2; Elizabeth Scalia, "'They Do Not Love Jesus,'" Patheos: Catholic Channel: The Anchoress, December 18, 2008, patheos.com/blogs/theanchoress/2008/12/18/they-do-not-love-jesus.

Week Four Group Discussion Guide

After completing Days 1–5 and reading the real life story, meet with your group. We offer this guide for your discussion.

PRAY (10 minutes)

Invite one or two volunteers to share persecution news stories they've read during the week. Pray for your spiritual family in these stories.

Ask the Lord also to increase your love, perhaps using Paul's prayer for the Philippian church as a model:

> This is my prayer: that your love may abound more and more in knowledge and depth of insight, so that you may be able to discern what is best and may be pure and blameless until the day of Christ, filled with the fruit of righteousness that comes through Jesus Christ—to the glory and praise of God. (Philippians 1:9–11)

SHARE (40 minutes)

Share with the group your thoughts and discoveries from the following questions:

Day 1, question 1

Day 2, questions 3 and 5

Day 3, question 1

Day 4, questions 1 and 2

Day 5, question 4

Share your thoughts about real life in India.

CLOSE (10 minutes)

Pray for the Christians in India. Ask the Lord to:

- Turn the heart of India's prime minister and other governmental leaders to allow God's people to worship Him peacefully.

- Grow and unify His church in India.

- Strengthen and encourage our brothers and sisters in India.

Pray for yourselves, that the Lord will strengthen the sincerity of your love and remove any impurity.

Ask for one or two volunteers who will take a few minutes during the week to read the latest persecution news and briefly share the news stories at your next meeting. Persecution news is available at *LumenLife.org/news*.

WEEK FIVE
Love Revived

"Let us consider how to stimulate one another to love and good deeds."
—Hebrews 10:24, NASB

Day 1   Heart Problems

Day 2   Unbroken Silence

Day 3   Spiritual CPR

Day 4   Band of Brothers

Day 5   A Heart for God = A Heart for His People

Day 6   Real Life in Pakistan: Rape of Innocence

Group Discussion Guide

Week Five

Day 1

Heart Problems

Use the following link to watch a one-minute introduction to *Heirloom Love* Week Five:

LumenLife.org/hlvideos

* * *

To more fully appreciate the impact of today's reading, take a few minutes to allow God's living and active Word to renew your mind. Equip yourself with His perspective as a clear lens for viewing current and recent events. Please read and meditate on John 13:34–35 and 17:20–23. Ask the Lord to open your heart and understanding to know and do His will.

* * *

In 1995, Ravi Zacharias summed up the American Christian response to persecution with the following statement: "Silence lurks where anguished voices should be heard."18 Zacharias said this during the first Sudanese holocaust, when Sudanese dictator Omar al-Bashir annihilated more than two million Christians during 1989–2005. American Christians responded with indifference to this sixteen-year genocide. The International Criminal Court has since indicted Bashir on three counts of genocide, five counts of crimes against humanity (murder, extermination, forcible transfer, torture and rape) and two counts of war crimes (pillaging and intentionally directing attacks against civilians).

---

18 Ravi Zacharias wrote these words in his afterword to Nina Shea, *In the Lion's Den* (Nashville: Broadman Holman, 1997).

Ravi Zacharias: "Silence lurks where anguished voices should be heard.

Also in 1995, Michael Horowitz published his earlier-mentioned op-ed *Wall Street Journal* article about Christian persecution. He cited several examples of "growing and large-scale persecution" of Christians. He described Christians as the Jews of the twenty-first century and challenged American Christians to speak up on behalf of their persecuted brothers and sisters. Mr. Horowitz's article influenced his longtime friend Dr. James Dobson to write the following in his "family news" letter from Focus on the Family:

> Most modern-day Christians in the affluent western nations seem utterly oblivious to the dire extremities to which Christians in Muslim and former Soviet nations are being pushed—with murder, rape, torture, slavery, imprisonment and confiscation of property growing at an exponential rate. . . .

> Michael Horowitz's original column in the *Wall Street Journal* should have generated an outpouring of support from outraged believers around the country. Inexplicably, it brought little more than a yawn.

Dr. Dobson also included this quotation from Nina Shea's *In the Lion's Den*: "Millions of American Christians pray in their churches each week, oblivious to the fact that Christians in many parts of the world suffer brutal torture, arrest, imprisonment and even death—their homes and communities laid waste—for no other reason than that they are Christians."

Dr. Dobson's letter continued:

> The shocking, untold story of our time is that more Christians have died this century simply for being Christians than in the first nineteen centuries after the birth of Christ. They have been persecuted before an unknowing, indifferent world and a largely silent Christian community.

Chuck Colson said, "When I see something like this, my heart aches because the believers here don't even know about it, don't care. We're not expressing moral outrage; we're not indignant of the indifference of the United States government towards this. And we ought to be marching in the streets because our brethren are being persecuted, imprisoned, beaten, sold into slavery, and butchered and we don't seem to care in this country."

In 1996, the National Association of Evangelicals (NAE) responded to

Horowitz, Dobson and Colson's challenge by issuing a "Statement of Conscience." In this statement the NAE, which represents forty-five thousand congregations from over forty different denominations across the United States, confessed their "silence" and "culpability." They pledged "to end today's wrongful silence by Christians . . . in the face of mounting persecution of Christian believers" and "to do what is within our power to address persecution." Several large denominations, including the Southern Baptist Convention, the Episcopal Church, the Presbyterian Church USA, and the United Methodist Church, also passed denominational resolutions and issued letters of support for the Statement of Conscience.

After issuing their statement, the NAE was instrumental in founding the International Day of Prayer for the Persecuted Church and lobbied for the formation of the USCRIF (United States Commission on International Religious Freedom)—a federal interfaith commission that is responsible for reviewing international violations of religious freedom and making policy recommendations to the president, the secretary of state and Congress.

But little has changed since then.

1. **Why do you think American Christians are seemingly indifferent toward the horrible mistreatment of Christians globally? Try to identify the specific reasons we fail to show that we care.**

2. **How might we correct the causes of apathy—in ourselves and in other Christians? What must we change to elevate our empathy?**

Week Five

Day 2

Unbroken Silence

Begin today by renewing your mind and vision with God's living Word, so you can proceed with His heart filling yours. Please read and meditate on 1 John 4:7–13. Ask the Lord to fill and guide you with His revolutionary love.

* * *

Not much has changed in the two decades since the NAE issued its Statement of Conscience. The USCRIF (United States Commission on International Religious Freedom) has been marginalized and virtually suffocated within the bowels of the State Department's bureaucracy. The US government does not necessarily follow the USCIRF's recommendations. For example, contrary to the USCRIF's recommendation, they did not include Nigeria or Pakistan on the commission's list of "Countries of Particular Concern," even though these countries are known to be among the worst perpetrators of heinous crimes and oppression against Christians.

The US provides tens of billions of dollars in foreign aid to countries like Pakistan, Nigeria and Egypt, where Christians are severely persecuted. The US government could leverage its foreign aid program to advance religious freedom. But it doesn't.

On June 5, 2011, Sudan's genocidal president, Omar al-Bashir, launched a second campaign to systematically annihilate Christians and other non-Muslims. From 2011 to 2017 Sudan's air force has conducted aerial bombardment of our brothers and sisters every single day, killing thousands in full view of the world.

Despite the International Criminal Court's multiple indictments against Bashir, despite his open continuation of his holocaust-like crimes against his own people, most world leaders—including many in the US—are idly watching. In 2011 the US

House Foreign Affairs Committee called for an emergency hearing to address this crisis. The State Department was conspicuously absent from the meeting. During the hearing, US Representative Frank Wolf (R-VA) said, "I think the church in the West really needs to do a better job of advocating for the persecuted church . . . the silence of the church in the West is absolutely incredible." British human rights activist Wilfred Wong confirms the root cause of our government's lack of support for persecuted Christians: "If Christians themselves do not have a deep awareness and concern for these issues, then it is hardly surprising when their governments fail to reflect such awareness or concern."[19]

> **"If Christians themselves do not have a deep awareness and concern for these issues, then it is hardly surprising when their governments fail to reflect such awareness or concern."**

In 2010 a US congressman sent letters to two hundred Christian and media leaders asking them to speak out on behalf of persecuted Christians. No one responded to the letter. When each of the leaders was contacted in follow-up, only one replied, saying, "We'll pray for you."

On September 27, 2013, Kristen Powers, in an article in the *Daily Beast*, commented on today's US Christian indifference to persecution:

> One would think this horror might be consuming the pulpits and pews of American churches. Not so. The silence has been nearly deafening. . . . American Christians are quite able to organize around issues that concern them. Yet religious persecution appears not to have grabbed their attention, despite worldwide media coverage of the atrocities against Christians and other religious minorities in the Middle East.[20]

During the week prior to the 2016 International Day of Prayer for the Persecuted Church, we reviewed the websites of the twenty largest denominations and two hundred largest churches in America. On their home pages, nearly all

---

[19] Interview of Wilfred Wong by Kim A. Lawton, Prague, Czech Republic, May 6, 1996.

[20] Kirsten Powers, "A Global Slaughter of Christians, but America's Churches Stay Silent," The Daily Beast, September 27, 2013, thedailybeast.com/articles/2013/09/27/a-global-slaughter-of-christians-but-america-s-churches-stay-silent.html.

of them advertised Veteran's Day or Thanksgiving-related "food for the hungry" programs. Only one of these websites mentioned the Day of Prayer for the Persecuted Church on their home page, and only eight of them listed it on their website's calendar of events or somewhere else on their websites.

Apparently I'm not the only American Christian guilty of ignoring the persecuted saints. Many of us are failing to understand Jesus' new command—its imperative nature and biblical application for the saints who are enduring the "fiery trial" of persecution.

* * *

Tom Catena is an American physician who is living sincere love in Sudan. Visit *LumenLife.org/Sudan* to meet Dr. Tom in a *New York Times* video. The victims in the video are mostly Christians who are being persecuted for their faith, even though the *New York Times* does not refer to them as such.

1. **We are unable to change our own hearts, to replace apathy with love. We need the Lord's help, and we must ask for it. Jesus' prayer for us, recorded in John 17, can guide us in praying for heart change. Considering today's widespread apathy toward the persecuted, what should we ask for ourselves and other Christians, according to:**

   John 17:11, 15?

   John 17:17–19?

   John 17:20–23?

   John 17:3, 24–26?

2. **Take a few minutes to pray for yourself and other American Christians as Jesus prayed for us. Record any meaningful thoughts that occur to you as you pray.**

Week Five

Day 3

Spiritual CPR

"When I heard these things, I sat down and wept. For some days I mourned and fasted and prayed before the God of heaven." (Nehemiah 1:4)

We know we should feel sad for the horrible things happening in other lands to our family in Christ. And sometimes, some of us do. But many of us don't.

The fact is that we can't manufacture genuine emotions on command. Genuine emotions arise from a heart of compassion that reflects God's burden for His people. We cultivate compassion when we gain an honest grasp of reality and engage it with a pure and open heart. If we don't experience sadness when we hear about our suffering spiritual siblings, it could be because we either don't have an intellectual understanding of their suffering or we're not allowing our hearts to become available and vulnerable enough to identify with them.

The first problem—failure to understand with our intellect—can be remedied simply by further exposure: Seek out reliable news of persecution, and be willing to listen to the painful details. But the second problem is more difficult to fix. Hardened hearts can't be penetrated by mere facts alone. To identify with our brothers and sisters at a heartfelt level, we must begin with prayer. We must be honest with the Lord about our lack of empathy or unwillingness to be involved, and He will help us to grow past it.

To identify with our brothers and sisters at a heartfelt level, we must begin with prayer.

In this attitude of submissive prayer, we can choose to engage our hearts and exercise our God-given imaginations to identify more closely with the persecuted. We can picture their faces and imagine the ways they're just like us. We can put ourselves in their place, imagining what they must feel and fear. We need to humble ourselves, to recognize that we could just as easily have been born in their country and their circumstances; we've done nothing to deserve our material blessings and our freedoms. And generally speaking, they've done nothing to deserve their impoverishment and pain. The Lord distributes advantage and agony as He sees fit, and we who are entrusted with liberty and earthly abundance bear a weight of accountability for the distribution of our many benefits.

Through both our conscious choices and the Lord's enabling transformation, we can learn to "rejoice with those who rejoice" and "weep with those who weep" (Romans 12:15, NASB). We will then exult in things that please the Lord and grieve for things that sadden Him—particularly for His children, suffering for His name.

It was with a desire for such change that I went before the Lord on August 25, 2009, asking Him to reveal His heart to me. I believe that I heard the word *Orissa*, as if whispered into my heart, in response to my prayer.

I was perplexed when I heard the word *Orissa*—the name of a state in India that I had encountered only once before, a year earlier, when I had learned that scores of Christians were killed by Hindu mobs who demanded they convert or be killed. Three hundred churches and six thousand Christian homes were looted and burnt down, and 56,000 Christians were left homeless.

I did some research and learned that more than ten thousand Christians in Orissa were still—one year after the attacks—homeless, living in the jungle, while nearly ten thousand more were living in conditions only slightly better, under tarps in squalid refugee camps. They dared not return to their homes, where Hindus were still abducting and threatening to kill Christians who refused to renounce their faith in Jesus.

I'm ashamed to admit I was not appropriately disturbed by what I learned. Twenty thousand of my Christian brothers and sisters in Orissa had been suffering and barely subsisting in the jungle and in refugee camps throughout the preceding year, and I was not genuinely troubled. But the softening of our hearts can take time, and the Lord is patient with us while we persist obediently toward His purposes.

1. Just as our physical heart is vital to our physical health, so also our spiritual "heart" is vital to our spiritual health. How would you honestly diagnose your spiritual heart? On a 1–10 scale (1 = "not at all," 10 = "completely"), how naturally do you rejoice in the things that please the Lord and mourn the things that grieve Him? Please explain.

2. Physicians advise reasonable diet and exercise for physical heart health. What are the dietary needs of your spiritual heart? How might you change what you see, hear, think for improved spiritual health? Answer in terms of your specific daily choices.

3. What kinds of exercise (practical acts of love and righteousness) will strengthen your inner person, making you more spiritually healthy? Answer in terms of your habitual daily words and actions.

Week Five

Day 4

Band of Brothers

In response to my prayers in 2009, I believe the Lord led me to read 2 Samuel 11 and Nehemiah 1–2. The Lord used the examples of two amazing men—Uriah and Nehemiah—to help me understand how godly men and women ought to respond in solidarity with our suffering brothers and sisters. We'll look at Uriah's story today and Nehemiah's tomorrow.

When we read the story of King David's sin with Bathsheba (2 Samuel 11), we naturally tend to focus on David. But let's review the story again, this time with careful attention to a different character—Bathsheba's husband, Uriah.

During wartime, David stayed home, away from the battle front. He saw Bathsheba bathing on her rooftop and sent for her, though she was married to one of his soldiers. They slept together and Bathsheba became pregnant. In a scheme to cover up his sin, David sent word to his general, Joab, to send Uriah back to Jerusalem with an update on the war. While Uriah was in Jerusalem he would certainly sleep with his wife—or so David thought—and her pregnancy would be attributed to him, not to David.

One problem: David did not plan for Uriah's love and loyalty to the Lord and his brothers.

David said to Uriah, "Go down to your house and wash your feet." So Uriah left the palace, and a gift from the king was sent after him. But Uriah slept at the entrance to the palace with all his master's servants and did not go down to his house.

When David was told, "Uriah did not go home," he asked him, "Haven't you just come from a distance? Why didn't you go home?"

Uriah said to David, "The ark and Israel and Judah are staying in tents, and my master Joab and my lord's men are camped in the open fields. How could I go to my house to eat and drink and lie with my wife? As surely as you live, I will not do such a thing!"

Then David said to him, "Stay here one more day, and tomorrow I will send you back." So Uriah remained in Jerusalem that day and the next. At David's invitation, he ate and drank with him, and David made him drunk. But in the evening Uriah went out to sleep on his mat among his master's servants; he did not go home. (2 Samuel 11:8–13)

Uriah didn't cooperate with David's cover-up, so David finally sent Uriah into a certain-death situation on the battlefront, where Uriah was killed.

Here was a man who identified so closely with his embattled, imperiled brothers that he refused the simple comforts of home when he had access to them. He could have gone home to his wife, but in solidarity with his brothers, he bunked in the servants' quarters, located at the palace entrance. Even the king's enticement couldn't persuade him to forget the glory of God and the well-being of his fellow soldiers.

At first glance, Uriah's situation might not seem very similar to ours. But make no mistake: Every believer in Jesus Christ is engaged in ongoing spiritual warfare. We are all fellow soldiers, and those who suffer for refusing to deny Jesus are among the bravest of the Lord's warriors.

Those who suffer for refusing to deny Jesus are among the bravest of the Lord's warriors.

We need to closely identify with these heroes on the battlefield. To cultivate solidarity with them, we must consciously recognize the true unity of all believers with each other in one body. In this awareness, we must purpose to engage in the spiritual war effort as godly fellow soldiers. This is the rightful duty of every true Christian. As we become more consistently engaged in the battle, we will naturally become even more mindful of our oneness with the persecuted and grow to love them like brothers in battle. Just as Uriah loved his fellow combatants.

It's this love and compassion that moves us to "remember the prisoners, as though in prison with them, and those who are ill-treated, since you yourselves also are in the body" (Hebrews 13:3, NASB). When we cultivate hearts like Uriah's, we hear of the Orissa crisis and think, *God's people are sheltering under tarps and trees, eating whatever they can find in the jungle. How can I go about my "normal life" as though they weren't there, suffering? I must help.*

1. Think about your spiritual family, your fellow soldiers on the front lines of the millennia-old spiritual war. What does "normal" mean for them? Picture someone who is suffering under persecution, and describe a normal day for him or her.

2. What habits can you develop to "correct your vision," to learn to see past your "normal" and keep in view the normal existence of your suffering brothers and sisters?

3. As you become more mindful of the unceasing embattlement of your dear spiritual siblings, how can you express your solidarity with them? What might you usefully give up on their behalf? How might you consciously change your "normal" in empathy with them—both to train your own heart and to support them?

Week Five

Day 5

A Heart for God = A Heart for His People

The other passage to which I sensed the Lord directing me was about another man with a heart after the Lord and a love for His people. Nehemiah was one of the Jewish exiles scattered throughout the Persian Empire after the Lord destroyed Israel as a kingdom. The Lord blessed Nehemiah's faithfulness and raised him to a position of influence and favor in the Persian emperor's court: He was the royal cupbearer. One day he welcomed some visitors who had just traveled from the homeland he had probably never seen.

> I questioned them about the Jewish remnant that survived the exile, and also about Jerusalem. They said to me, "Those who survived the exile and are back in the province are in great trouble and disgrace. The wall of Jerusalem is broken down, and its gates have been burned with fire."

> When I heard these things, I sat down and wept. For some days I mourned and fasted and prayed before the God of heaven. Then I said: "O Lord, God of heaven . . . let your ear be attentive and your eyes open to hear the prayer your servant is praying before you day and night for your servants. . . . They are your servants and your people, whom you redeemed by your great strength and your mighty hand. O Lord, let your ear be attentive to the prayer of this your servant and to the prayer of your servants who delight in revering your name. Give your servant success today by granting him favor in the presence of this man." (Nehemiah 1:2–6, 10–11)

This prayer was six months in the making—from the fall of the year, when Nehemiah received the distressing news, to one day the next spring—the day he would petition the king for permission to go and help his people. "I was serving the king his wine. I had never before appeared sad in his presence. So the king asked me, 'Why are you looking so sad? You don't look sick to me. You must be deeply troubled.' Then I was terrified, but I replied, 'Long live the king! How can I not be sad?'" (Nehemiah 2:1–3, NLT).

Nehemiah went on to explain his grief. The Lord had planted such a love for Nehemiah in the king's heart that the king gladly granted Nehemiah's every request, including letters of passage and even a mounted military unit for protection.

**When I heard these things, I sat down and wept.
For some days I mourned and fasted and prayed before
the God of heaven.**

As I read Nehemiah's story, the Lord was drawing my attention to the example of a broken-hearted, godly man. Much as I had inquired of my Christian siblings in Orissa, Nehemiah had inquired about the welfare of his countrymen back in Judah. The circumstances for God's people in devastated Jerusalem were similar to the Christians' plight in twenty-first-century Orissa. In both situations His people were "in great trouble" or "great distress" (NASB), having been driven from their burning homes.

The greatest *dis*similarity in this comparison was between Nehemiah's response and mine. I was beginning to feel compassion—the Holy Spirit was starting to soften my heart—but Nehemiah spontaneously slumped and wept. Such was the relationship he had already cultivated with the Lord, and such was his affinity with God's people. His first several days of mourning, fasting and prayer stretched into months; half a year later his sorrow was so obvious that the leader of the world power took notice.

Centuries before Christ's advent, Nehemiah modeled what it means to "bear one another's burdens, and thereby fulfill the law of Christ" (Galatians 6:2, NASB). He embodied the principle that when "one member suffers, all the members suffer with it" (1 Corinthians 12:26, NASB). Nehemiah's faith and love proved to be genuine because they moved him to action and sacrifice. He risked the emperor's disfavor—a prospect never to be taken lightly!—in order to come to his people's aid. His response to his brothers' crisis was "Send me."

As we seek and know the Lord, our affections will come into line with His. If we remain mindful of our solidarity with God's people, our emotions will more and more naturally become what they should be. Keep practicing faithful dependence on the Lord, and your love will grow. And the outflow will be an increasing current of fervent love, prayer, action and sacrifice for our persecuted brothers and sisters.

"As for the saints who are in the earth, They are the majestic ones in whom is all my delight." (Psalm 16:3, NASB)

1. **What makes you weep? Take a few minutes and conduct an honest heart check. Our emotions—our joy and our sadness—are often a reflection of what we treasure. We mourn for the loss of whatever genuinely matters to us. What do you treasure most and most fear losing?**

2. **Ask Nehemiah's question of yourself: "How can I not be sad?" As we learn to delight in the Lord's "majestic ones," we'll naturally cultivate a heart of compassion that grieves for their suffering. How might you adjust what you treasure and honor as valuable?**

Week Five

Day 6

Real Life in Pakistan

RAPE OF INNOCENCE

Anna isn't her real name, but in every important way on that Friday morning she was just like any other twelve-year-old girl of any name. She played. She dreamed. She laughed and cried. She was young enough still to harbor elements of a child's innocent outlook upon the world.

She was young enough to trust.

It was Christmas Eve, and Anna's home, like most Christian homes in Lahore, Pakistan, was probably decorated inside with locally crafted trinkets and a tree, and outside with a "star of Bethlehem" on the roof. Perhaps during the preceding week she had participated in caroling from home to home, or maybe she'd given coins rewarding carolers who had come to her home. She was certainly anticipating the celebration that would begin that midnight, as well as the church services and family gatherings of Christmas Day itself.

That Christmas Eve morning a Muslim neighbor girl—one of Anna's friends—came by and invited Anna to go shopping. Together they headed out. Maybe Anna contemplated buying gifts for her family: special Christmas treats or a decoration for the house. Her friend led her to a car occupied by two strange Muslim men, one of whom the friend introduced as her uncle. The girls got into the car.

We can only imagine at what point Anna realized her shopping trip was turning into something else. Maybe it was when the car left familiar territory and continued on. Maybe it was when she was warned to keep silent. Maybe it was when she was led—perhaps naively, or perhaps against her will—into a strange house.

Over the next two days multiple men raped her. And her ordeal had only begun.

Keep in mind: Anna was *twelve years old.*

On the day after Christmas, three women and Anna's "friend" came to her, promising her release if she would sign some papers. Only the promise of freedom convinced her to sign. She didn't realize that she had just "consented" to marry one of her rapists, a man named Muhammad Irfan.

Anna was never released. For more than eight months she was kept imprisoned, moved from place to place, and repeatedly raped. She was forced to convert to Islam in order to become a suitable wife. When she insisted on remaining faithful to Jesus Christ, she was beaten. By Islamic teaching, her refusal was no barrier to her being made a Muslim, and she was forced to marry Muhammad Irfan.

Anna's family, frantic to find their daughter, had no idea who had kidnapped her. So they filed a complaint "against unknown people" with local police in Lahore. The police took no action. After all, these were only Christians.

Finally, in early September, Anna escaped her captors. She hid out at a bus stop and called her parents from a public telephone. The family traveled more than a hundred miles to Faisalabad to retrieve her. Back in Lahore they brought Anna before a local magistrate, who recorded Anna's statement, but refused to assign protection or even to order a medical exam for Anna.

The rapists—shamelessly unafraid of being identified—appealed to police, presenting a marriage certificate as "proof " that Anna was now a Muslim and married to one of the group. Now equipped with the names of the criminals, Anna's family returned to the police to amend their formal complaint to include the perpetrators' names. The response: No. We won't let you do that. In fact, you need to be reasonable. Everyone concerned will be better off when you return the girl to her "legal" husband. If you don't, you'll be considered criminals; a case will be filed against you.

All this despite the fact that Pakistani law forbids marriage under age sixteen—as well as kidnapping, rape, beatings and false accusation.

Since then, according to the latest available records, neither Anna nor her family have been able to return to their home; they're on the run from her captors, from the police, and possibly from a terrorist group with whom her rapists are allegedly associated. If the family is found, they could lose their freedom or their lives.

What if you were Anna's mother or father, or her brother or sister? Consider for a moment what these circumstances mean for these very real people, treated in these ways simply because they choose to love Jesus. They've left behind their home, their possessions, their friends, their way of life. What would these losses mean to you?

And what about Anna? Hopeless and violated for what seemed like eternity, is she afraid to close her eyes because of the horrors that fill her dreams at night? The emotional barriers that now hinder her from ever accepting herself or trusting a man must seem insurmountable. Will she ever believe she's worth anything, or will she see herself as forever ruined, destined merely to endure the deep lonely ache throughout her remaining days, years, decades?

The word *tragedy* seems too tame to describe Anna's ordeal and its aftermath. But her story is happening all over Pakistan to other Annas. In this country where women have especially low social status, some estimate that seven hundred Christian girls and women each year are kidnapped, raped, forcibly converted to Islam and forcibly married to their captors. Since 99 percent of rape cases in Pakistan are never reported,[21] the actual number of victims is probably many times that conservative estimate. Every year. Year after year.

One Muslim cleric, while solemnizing a forced marriage, declared the rapist's behavior to be "a pious act" because he had "saved" his victim, bringing her into Islam. When the Christian father of a sixteen-year-old rape victim complained to police, he was kidnapped, shackled, tortured and left in critical condition. In one village in Punjab Province, when Christians objected "too strenuously" to the daily sexual assaults on their women and girls, Muslim leaders ordered 250 Christian families to leave the village and their homes. (The village was first founded by Christians around 1950.)

This disturbing and increasing practice of sexual predation is only one of many tools used by the Muslim majority in Pakistan to persecute Christ's followers there. Homes and property may be seized. Christians are often discriminated against and harassed at their places of work. And Christian students are often publicly ridiculed and even beaten, simply because they love Jesus.

---

[21] According to the president of the Pakistan Christian Congress.

Among the weapons wielded against Christians in Pakistan are its often misused blasphemy laws. Many Muslims, wishing to settle personal vendettas against Christians, have manufactured blasphemy lawsuits against them. These laws include statutes that prohibit "injuring religious feelings," "defiling the Quran" and "blaspheming Muhammad." The first two carry a maximum penalty of life imprisonment, and the last a possible death sentence.

Imagine yourself a follower of Jesus in Pakistan. You read in God's Word that faithfulness to Him means not just worshipping Him and following His example, but also telling others about Jesus and His love. But obeying the Lord's Commission is to risk the possibility of being charged with blasphemy against Islam. Imagine this uncertain daily existence for those who seek to live in faithfulness and obedience to the Lord.

Hundreds of thousands of Christians in Pakistan are so impoverished they're virtual slaves, indebted to Muslim landlords. When they encounter persecution or are accused of breaking some law, few can afford to miss a day of work to go to court, let alone afford the cost of an attorney. One way desperate Christians raise money is by selling one of their kidneys; they're exploited by a burgeoning illegal transplant industry in the country. Thousands of Christians are believed to have sold kidneys to pay off debts. But often the money promised to the donor is unpaid or paid only in part; often unskilled surgeons perform the operations and patients cannot afford proper follow-up care. Many Christians who take this dangerous risk fall seriously ill and die. Let us give thanks for our liberty and remember our brothers and sisters in Pakistan, enduring impossible circumstances simply to survive in one of the world's most hostile and oppressive countries toward Christians.

And especially at Christmas, remember Anna, whose dream Christmas became a nightmare. Pray that she and thousands of girls and women like her might find protection, healing and peace in their heavenly Protector's arms.

Pray that Anna might laugh again.[22]

---

[22] Sources: "Pakistan: A 12-Year-Old Christian Is Gang-Raped for Eight Months, Forcibly Converted and Then 'Married' to Her Muslim Attacker," Asian Human Rights Commission, October 10, 2011, humanrights.asia/news/urgent-appeals/AHRC-UAC-199–2011; Ali Usman, "Cash for Kidneys: Pakistan's Flourishing Trade in Illegal Transplants," *Express Tribune,* July 23, 2012, tribune.com.pk/story/411570/cash-for-kidneys-pakistans-flourishing-trade-in-illegaltransplants.

Week Five Group Discussion Guide

After completing Days 1–5 and reading the real life story, meet with your group. We offer this guide for your discussion.

PRAY (10 minutes)

Share the latest persecution news stories. Then pray for your spiritual family in those true stories.

Ask the Lord to burden your hearts with His concerns and to open your minds to His truth. Pray for each other's growth in submission to Him and for a deeper love relationship with Him.

SHARE (40 minutes)

Share with the group your thoughts and discoveries from the following questions:

Day 1, questions 1 and 2

Day 2, question 1

Day 3, questions 2 and 3

Day 4, question 3

Day 5, question 2

Share your thoughts about real life in Pakistan.

CLOSE (10 minutes)

Pray for the Christians in Pakistan. Ask the Lord to:

- Repeal the blasphemy laws that are used to falsely accuse and imprison Christians.
- Release the millions of slaves in Pakistan, many of whom are Christians.
- Strengthen and grow His church in Pakistan.

Pray for yourselves, for hearts and minds devoted fully to God's kingdom, and for His great joy as your reward.

Ask one or two volunteers to take a few minutes during the upcoming week to read the latest persecution news and briefly share the news stories at your next group meeting. Persecution news is available at *LumenLife.org/news*.

WEEK SIX

Love Proven

"Show these men the proof of your love . . . so that the churches can see it."
—Paul to the Corinthian church, 2 Corinthians 8:24

Day 1   Awareness: Open Your Mind

Day 2   Prayer: Open Your Heart

Day 3   Advocacy: Open Your Mouth

Day 4   Relief and Development: Open Your Hand

Day 5   Let Brotherly Love Continue

Day 6   Real Life in Nigeria: A Year in Memoriam

Group Discussion Guide

Week Six

Day 1

Awareness: Open Your Mind

Use the following link to watch a one-minute introduction to Week Six of your journey to heirloom love:

LumenLife.org/hlvideos

* * *

Spend a few minutes reviewing and once again pondering the following Scripture passages about genuine faith and love:

A new command I give you: Love one another. As I have loved you, so you must love one another. (Jesus in John 13:34)

What good is it, my brothers, if a man claims to have faith but has no deeds? Can such faith save him? Suppose a brother or sister is without clothes and daily food. If one of you says to him, "Go, I wish you well; keep warm and well fed," but does nothing about his physical needs, what good is it? In the same way, faith by itself, if it is not accompanied by action, is dead. (James 2:14–17)

Above all things have fervent love for one another (1 Peter 4:8, NKJV).

This is how we know what love is: Jesus Christ laid down his life for us. And we ought to lay down our lives for our brothers. If anyone has material possessions and sees his brother in need but has no pity on him, how can the love of God be in him? Dear children, let us not love with words or tongue but with actions and in truth. (1 John 3:16–18)

1. Summarize your previous study of these passages. What is *and is not* genuine faith in God and love for others?

I speak on behalf of my brethren who lie in countless nameless graves. I speak on behalf of my brethren who now meet secretly in forests, basements, attics, and other such places.

The message I bring from the Underground Church is:

"Don't abandon us!"

"Don't forget us!"

"Don't write us off!"

"Give us the tools we need! We will pay the price for using them!"

This is the message I have been charged to deliver to the free Church. I speak for the Underground Church, the silenced Church, the "dumb" Church, which has no voice to speak.

—Richard Wurmbrand, *Tortured for Christ*

Throughout this book, in some words or other, we've heard the same message from Jesus, from John, from James and from Paul: *You say you love? Prove it!* "Show these men the proof of your love . . . so that the churches can see it" (2 Corinthians 8:24).

Our love for Jesus and our brothers and sisters in the body of Christ has to be more than a profession—it must produce action. Words alone are worse than weak; they're worthless. Nobel Peace Prize nominee Mama Maggie Gobran said the same: "When you love somebody—you live it."[23]

---

[23] Mama Maggie Gobran led a comfortable life in Cairo as a Christian from a prominent Egyptian family before following a conviction from God to serve the poorest-of-the-poor Christian children and families who, due to persecution and oppression, have been forced to live in an active landfill—often referred to as "Garbage City."

One high-priority means by which the Lord requires that we demonstrate our love is to minister to persecuted Christians. And you don't have to travel overseas. There's much you can do to help right in your home or church.

Our love for Jesus and our brothers and sisters in the body of Christ has to be more than a profession—it must produce action.

Action on behalf of our needy family will look different for each of us. A good starting place is to confirm a right attitude—to seek and commit your ways to the One who is moving your heart. Follow the Macedonians' lead and give yourself first to the Lord (see 2 Corinthians 8:5). When you commit to full submission to Him, you will more readily discover good action steps, along with a greater eagerness to take them.

Let me suggest a four-part action plan that is based on Nehemiah's example. First, he took a proactive interest in the circumstances and relevant events affecting his people (1:2). Second, when Nehemiah heard the news about his brothers' circumstances, he "fasted and prayed before the God of heaven" (1:4). Third, Nehemiah advocated on behalf of his brothers and sisters (2:3–8). And fourth, he ministered practically to his people's physical needs—carrying out fundraising activities and donating from his own wealth (5:14–19; 7:70). Similarly, each of us is able in our own way to prove our love for the persecuted saints through one or more of these responses:

- Awareness
- Prayer
- Advocacy
- Relief and development

As part of my own heirloom love journey, the Lord led me to start a ministry called LumenLife. This ministry is designed to provide people like you with information, tools and assistance to help you remember, pray for and care for our persecuted brothers and sisters in Christ. Throughout the rest of Week Six you will see references and links to resources on the LumenLife website in all four of these areas of compassionate action.

* * *

The first way we can prove our love for the persecuted is simply by seeking to know about their circumstances. We demonstrate the proof of our love by taking an active interest in the issues and events that affect them.

Have you ever gone through a difficult trial and had someone else—maybe even a stranger—ask with genuine interest about how you're doing in that circumstance? Even if they couldn't do anything else to help, your spirits were lifted just by knowing that someone cared enough to inquire. You knew you weren't alone. In the same way, our pursuit of awareness about our suffering spiritual siblings is an important expression of love and a meaningful ministry to those who suffer.

Even more, awareness is a prerequisite to any other measures we might take to help. We need to know about specific circumstances and needs before we can respond effectively with the other three categories of support—prayer, advocacy and assistance. For example, if we seek awareness of current events in India, we would learn that Indian lawmakers (at the time of this writing) are proposing laws that would effectively make it illegal for Christians to talk about their faith. This would be devastating for our thirty million Indian brothers and sisters, having to risk prison for obedience to Christ. This awareness guides us to pray specifically that these laws would not be passed.

If we seek awareness of current events in Sudan, we would know that President al-Bashir still has his sites set on "cleansing" Sudan of all remaining Christians, just as Haman had hoped to annihilate the Jews in the biblical story of Esther. Out of this awareness would naturally emerge our further expressions of love—including our informed, fervent petitions to the Lord to save and change al-Bashir's heart and, if necessary, bring him to justice, as the Lord did to Haman in response to the prayers of Esther and her people.

Christian persecution is complicated. Approximately two hundred million Christians around the world are being persecuted by various religions and numerous governments. It can be daunting to know where to start. The important first step is to regularly read the news, asking the Lord to direct you to a specific region or country that you can adopt. By focusing your research, you can become an expert on the details and intricacies of the oppressors, their laws and tactics, the needs of local Christians and the ministries that are serving them. You might even adopt a church in a persecuted country!

The world does not share our passion and concern for God's children. Nor should we expect them to. As we've seen, we cannot count on the world and its media to provide us with current, complete and accurate information on Christian persecution.

We must seek and use alternate sources for news—most of which are available through the Internet—to learn about the needs and circumstances of our persecuted family. Several organizations exist with connections to reliable, first-hand, in-country sources throughout the world—organizations committed to disseminating the disturbing truth in order to stir us to action and intervention. They're doing their part in order that we might do ours. Visit their websites, including our own *LumenLife.org/news*. Appendix C in this book includes a list of ministries that provide news, guidance for prayer, advocacy or relief for persecuted Christians. Sign up for their news feeds, follow them on social media, place links to these websites on yours, and take other action to gain information and to make information available to others. Persecution news should be made a priority in our homes and churches. It should receive prime placement on church websites, in bulletins and in other communications. Every church should designate one or more "ambassadors" responsible for providing regular news updates to their local church.

* * *

Picture some of your suffering fellow believers, whom you've "met" throughout this study. See their faces. Speak their names. Describe their circumstances. What will it mean to them simply to discover your interest? With these *real* souls in mind . . .

2. **What steps will you take to learn and stay informed about brothers and sisters suffering right now for Jesus? Consider choosing a partner for sharing and accountability.**

3. **How might you become a persecution news source to others in your church and among family and friends? How might you guide and support others to help spread the latest news?**

Week Six

Day 2

Prayer: Open Your Heart

The second activity that proves our love is prayer on behalf of the persecuted. When Nehemiah had received the sorrowful report about the Lord's people and their city, he "wept, mourned and fasted and prayed before the God of heaven" (Nehemiah 1:4). He persisted in expectant prayer for six months before the Lord's answer came.

I recall a time when I was feeling helpless and overwhelmed by the widescale nature and intensity of global persecution. I prayed and asked the Lord what I could possibly do to help my brothers and sisters. In my spirit I clearly heard the command, *Pray*. So I began to pray for the safety of Christians in Indonesia and Nigeria. I later read that about the same time I was praying, three thousand pounds of explosives were found next to a church in Indonesia. The explosives had been placed next to a gas main at the side of the church, but a mechanical failure kept them from exploding. Praise the Lord! I also read that about this time a bomb was thrown into a Nigerian church during a service, but it failed to detonate.

I'm not suggesting my prayers were the sole reason these bombs did not explode. However, I do believe the Lord was teaching me that we can make an important difference for our brothers and sisters in danger, prison and affliction . . . simply by remembering them in our prayers. Why do so many of us fail to pray for the persecuted? For some, our silence before the Lord's throne might be rooted in ignorance and indifference. When I recognized this in myself, I began by confessing my indifference and made the conscious decision to begin regularly reading persecution news. This step alone caused my compassion and prayers to increase considerably.

Among other things, our prayers for the saints in tribulation should include the following petitions:

- That through them, the Lord's Word and reputation will spread rapidly, and He will be glorified (2 Thessalonians 3:1)
- That those who oppose them might come to salvation in Christ
- That the Lord would comfort them and grant them spiritual maturity, endurance, provision and protection
- That they will be mercifully delivered from perverse and evil men (2 Thessalonians 3:2)

You can find more guidance for your prayers in Appendix D of this book. As you pray, *watch!* Keep your eyes open for the Lord's answers. Watch for prisoners who are released, for governments that fall or change policy and for Christians who are allowed to return safely to their homes. And even when difficult circumstances don't change—or become worse—*listen!* Listen for the glowing testimonies of faith and love, honed and strengthened under unimaginable pressure and stress. Be humbled by these examples of Spirit-enabled fortitude, learn from them, and keep praying.

Over recent years the informed prayers of Christians around the world bolstered the faith of a twenty-seven-year-old Sudanese woman named Meriam Ibrahim. She and her mother had been abandoned by her Muslim father when she was young, and her mother raised her in the Christian faith. By God's grace, Meriam trusts and loves Jesus.

Meriam married Daniel Wani, a Christian and US citizen. Daniel is confined to a wheelchair with muscular dystrophy. Together, they have a two-year-old son, Martin. On May 15, 2014, Meriam was eight months pregnant with their second child when her faith was severely tested. She was arrested and convicted of adultery because Sudan wouldn't recognize her marriage to a Christian. She was also convicted of apostasy—for supposedly abandoning the Muslim faith of her long-gone father. Her so-called "adulterous" marriage earned her a sentence of one hundred lashes. Her "apostasy"—her all-out love for her Lord—drew a sentence of death by hanging. The lashes were postponed until she recovered from giving birth, and her execution until she weaned her baby. Meriam gave birth to Maya while in shackles and chains. Both of her children were kept in prison with her, even though they are Americans by virtue of their father's citizenship.

At one point, Sudanese Judge Mohammed Al-Khalifa gave Meriam the opportunity to abandon Jesus Christ and return to Islam. Our sister faced the gravest decision of her life: What would she love more—her life or her Lord? Was her commitment to Jesus strong enough that she could leave her children motherless and her wheelchair-bound husband a widower? Would she trade her remaining natural days on earth for an early entrance into eternal glory?

Meriam faced the man who seemingly held her physical destiny in his hands. With strength born of many prayers, she proclaimed her steadfast commitment to Him who had granted her eternal life. Heaven rejoiced, and God was glorified.

Thousands of Meriams and Daniels around the world are depending on and desperate for your prayers for strength and courage. Imagine what will happen when more of us—tens of thousands, even millions of us!—begin praying regularly and fervently, equipped and guided by accurate information about current events around the world. What might happen when we, like Nehemiah, begin fasting and crying out together for, say, the North Korean children of God? What might the Lord, the Authority who governs all authorities, do in the hearts and circumstances of leaders like Kim Jong-un, the dictator in that country? When He's ready, the Creator can at once annihilate that corrupt government—or redirect a tyrant's heart and mind.

Imagine the Lord's perspective at this moment on our prayers for the perse-cuted—on the resounding silence on this topic emanating from so many of our prayer closets. Currently, He hears a whisper here, a mutter there from across the Western world. But what if the whispers multiplied and spread? What if the tiny trickle swelled to a stream, then a torrent? What if mediocre souls began to burn with desperate, confident fervor, and muttering gave way to shouts of vicarious pain, then victory?

* * *

Imagine how interested, prayerful and active you would be if your own biolog-ical family members were being unjustly punished or imprisoned in a foreign country. Picture your mother or father, your son or daughter, your brother or sister suffering at the hand of some oppressor overseas. Would you ever stop praying? To what other lengths would you go on their behalf? This is how engaged we should be in fervent prayer and action on behalf of our persecuted brothers and sisters, "as though in prison with them" (Hebrews 13:3, NASB).

Imagine how interested, prayerful and active you would be if your own biological family members were being unjustly punished or imprisoned

---

1. What new step will you take to expand your prayer efforts for suffering Christians? Consider choosing a partner to keep each other faithful in prayer.

2. How might you lead and support others to grow in prayer for the persecuted?

Week Six

Day 3

Advocacy: Open Your Mouth

Meditate on Proverbs 31:8–9 (NASB):

> Open your mouth for the mute,
> for the rights of all the unfortunate.
> Open your mouth, judge righteously,
> and defend the rights of the afflicted and needy.

1. **After this life, when the Lord requires your accounting for how you used your voice for the voiceless, how do you want to be able to respond?**

The proof of our love is also seen in our willingness to speak on behalf of our brothers and sisters whose voices cannot be heard. True love cannot remain silent while those we say we love are being tortured and killed for our common faith.

Congressman Frank Wolf once gave a speech in which he quoted Chinese human rights lawyers, who said "that their lives improve, and those of their cohorts in prison or facing other pressures by the Chinese government, when the West speaks out for their plight and raises their cases by name."[24] In an interview with the *Christian Post*, Congressman Wolf was asked if it helps when people advocate for those being persecuted. He answered,

> It always helps. Every dissident always told me that, when people advocate for them, it improves conditions. If you are a dissident in prison and people start sending letters to the government or even to the commandant of the camp, your life gets better. . . . Sometimes it helps them get out of prison, or they get a little more food. Always stand with them because it really makes a big difference.

According to Christian Solidarity Worldwide,

> Lobbying to influence decision makers has in the past resulted in dramatic improvement for prisoners and victims of religious persecution. Torture has been stopped, access to doctors or lawyers has been granted, death sentences have been overturned and prisoners have been released. All governments, even the most repressive ones, dislike bad publicity because they depend on claiming legitimacy and authority. Exposing the illegal and inhumane acts of repressive regimes damages their trade, their tourism and their world standing.

While we're petitioning our Lord in prayer, we need also to petition our government, the United Nations and other world leaders to exert their substantial influence to change specific persecution situations. The mainstream media isn't going to raise awareness. That's our job.

You'll recall Meriam Ibraham, our Sudanese sister in Christ, whose story you read in Day 2. While she awaited her flogging and execution, news of Meriam's difficulties "went viral" worldwide, and people spoke. Countless thousands of emails, phone calls and written petitions bombarded politicians to pressure Sudan to release this innocent, Jesus-adoring woman and her two children.

We need also to petition our government, the United Nations and other world leaders.

---

[24] Frank Wolf, "Obama Administration Needs to 'Find Its Voice' on Human Rights," The Hill, July 26, 2010, thehill.com/blogs/congressblog/foreign-policy/110849-obama-administration-needs-to-find-itsvoice-on-human-rights-rep-frank-wolf.

Meriam's plight prompted me to take steps I had never taken before. My conscience would not allow me to remain silent. With help from some friends, LumenLife created a Rescue Meriam website and Facebook page to keep people updated about our sister, to offer a petition people could e-sign, and to help them electronically send letters on Meriam's behalf to both US and Sudanese officials. Because Meriam gave birth to baby Maya in the notorious Omdurman Prison, we launched a campaign to encourage individuals and churches to send birthday cards in pink envelopes to the Sudanese prison. We didn't expect Meriam to receive the cards, but the flood of pink envelopes was a timely and not-so-welcome reminder to the Sudanese officials that the world was watching their regime.

We initiated a demonstration in Washington, DC, to raise awareness of Meriam's case. We coordinated with other organizations, and at the one-day event we had hundreds of people carrying signs in front of the White House. Several congressmen came and spoke for Meriam. *Time*, *ABC News*, *FOX News* and many others picked up the demonstration and Meriam's story.

I arrived in Washington two days early and demonstrated in front of the Sudanese Embassy, joined at first by one other person I didn't know. By the second day we had drawn a team of thirty. I carried a sign offering to take Meriam's lashes. Of course, my main objective was to raise awareness of Sudan's cruelty toward women. But my offer was real—I would have taken Meriam's lashes if necessary.

The negative publicity worked. Before our demonstration the US State Department had refused to comment on Meriam's case. But within twenty-four hours of our event they issued a statement condemning Sudan's treatment of Meriam. About the same time Christians in other countries were also demonstrating on Meriam's behalf, which led other world governments also to pressure Sudan to release Meriam. And today Meriam, Daniel and their children live and worship freely in the United States.

I'm trying to make two points. First, advocacy works. When good people spoke out, the Lord responded by moving the hearts of presidents and kings. Governments took notice and began to reprimand the Sudanese government. My second point: I had never done anything like this before. I went way out of my comfort zone. If I can do it, you can too!

LumenLife includes, as part of our mission, the active advocacy for persecuted Christians around the world. We and several other of the organizations listed in Appendix C are exercising our voice toward this end and offer online advocacy tools to anyone willing to add their voices as well. We're providing information, guidance and technology to ensure that our concerned voices can be heard by authorities in our own country and around the world.

Don't forget that social media sharing can be caring. This is a highly effective way to amplify your voice on behalf of our voiceless brothers and sisters. We used Facebook and Twitter extensively to elevate Meriam's case and many others in our spiritual family.

I've talked to many churches with international social justice and advocacy ministries for important causes, such as human trafficking. I didn't find one church that was pleading the cause of the afflicted saints. I suspect a few are out there somewhere, but I haven't found them. Every year, thousands of young teenage Christian girls in countries like Pakistan and Egypt are kidnapped, raped and forced to marry Muslim men, and then become slaves for the rest of their lives. Why aren't we speaking up for them and the countless other Christians who are unjustly imprisoned, tortured, beaten, enslaved and oppressed? Our persecuted brothers and sisters are like sheep being herded helplessly to slaughter.

We can make a difference! We must break our silence and show the proof of our love.

2. **When have you been helpless because no one listened to you? When has someone spoken on your behalf?**

3. **Find one simple way you can exercise your freedom and influence to speak for your suffering brothers and sisters. Email the US president or secretary of state or your legislators, urging them to defend the human rights of Christians and other minorities around the world. Bring to their attention specific violations of human rights.**

4. **How will you bring these needs and opportunities to the awareness of your family, friends and church, so they can add their voices?**

Week Six

Day 4

Relief and Development: Open Your Hand

Take a moment to ponder Matthew 24:45–46, instructions to us from the mouth of Jesus, our King:

> Who then is the faithful and wise servant, whom the master has put in charge of the servants in his household to give them their food at the proper time? It will be good for that servant whose master finds him doing so when he returns.

1. When your King returns and asks, "Did you take care of My servants, your brothers and sisters in My family?" how do you want to answer? (Consider also Matthew 25:31–46.)

Finally, the proof of our genuine love will be visible (or not) in our checkbook registers and bank statements. Millions of persecuted believers around the world need assistance from us, their brothers and sisters who have been entrusted with liberty and abundance. Many of us in the US have "the goods of this world" (1 John 3:17, NASB). We are therefore responsible to "share with God's people who are in need" by providing for their physical needs (Romans 12:13; see also James 2:16).

In this day of globally available information we can all "see our brother in need," to adapt the words of John (1 John 3:17). Although we may not literally *see* the persecuted, we know about them, and John's instruction—and Jesus' new command—still holds us accountable for the information readily available to us concerning our spiritual family's suffering. Righteousness requires that awareness or access to information must lead to action.

The proof of our genuine love will be visible (or not) in our checkbook registers and bank statements.

Here are just a few of the ways we can help through financial support:

1. Providing for believers who have been forced to leave behind their homes, possessions and livelihoods, who are now dependent on the body of Christ for food, clothing and shelter.

2. Helping women and children in distress (James 1:27) because their husbands and fathers have been murdered or imprisoned for their faith. These incarcerated and murdered men are often church leaders, and they usually represent the only source of income for their already impoverished families.

3. Rescuing the millions of believers who are forced, expressly because of their faith, to live in literal garbage dumps and other putrid environments. They are denied access to housing, education and reasonable employment that would sustain their families.

4. Providing costly medical assistance for believers who have been tortured and beaten.

5. Providing legal assistance for Christians who have been unjustly treated, falsely accused and imprisoned. These believers are often already impoverished before their arrest, and in prison they're unable to work to support their families, let alone to pay legal fees.

Numerous organizations minister to the physical needs of suffering people around the world. Only a few organizations specialize in ministering to persecuted Christians. Don't assume that an organization's aid is targeted toward persecuted Christians; ask them.

And research the integrity and effectiveness of organizations to whom you're considering giving. One person, after reading *Heirloom Love,* informed me that they were compelled to give one-half of their retirement to help feed the needy in the household of faith. They were ready to send the money to an organization, until I told them that only 15 percent of this ministry's donations were spent on food for the intended beneficiaries.

Ministry to persecuted Christians is complex and dangerous work—dangerous for both the helping organization and for the recipients. This type of ministry usually must be conducted discreetly through trusted indigenous churches and partners who can deliver aid under the radar, undetected by watchful adversaries. Several of the organizations listed in Appendix C specialize in and have a proven ability to effectively provide aid to persecuted Christians. I encourage you to generously support these types of organizations. Or you can send tax-deductible donations to LumenLife, where we commit to use 100 percent of all funds received to benefit the persecuted body of Christ. For additional information on this, go to *LumenLife.org/donations*

* * *

Even the poor in the US have something to share with millions of Jesus followers, dying or deprived by starvation, illness, exposure, and mistreatment. A few dollars can mean life for families robbed of their homes, shivering under a tree or a tarp. For those who eat one handful of grain per day, or less, while their oppressors thrive.

2. **Does your spending and lifestyle already prove the sincerity of your love? If not, what changes will you make for the sake of love? Where do you spend money that you could save and give to help those who are suffering for the name of Jesus Christ?**

3. Practically speaking, how is the Lord leading you to share your abundance with persecuted brothers and sisters in true poverty? If this is new to you, consider just a small step to start. And consider choosing a partner for encouragement and accountability.

4. How might you infect others with the grace and joy of sharing?

Week Six

Day 5

Let Brotherly Love Continue

When we take action, it will look different for each of us. God has given everyone the ability to serve our needy family in a special way (see 1 Peter 4:10–11). I've shared several ideas in Days 1–4. Here are a few more:

One of the most important and effective things you can do to help our persecuted family is start an Heirloom Love small group with your friends or church. This way you can become part of the Lord's work reviving American Christianity, radically multiplying the number of people who are caring for the persecuted. In groups, members can support and encourage each other toward faithful obedience. Ask your leader for information about starting an Heirloom Love group.

Start an Heirloom Love small group

Signing the Heirloom Love Confession is a great way to help solidify your intentions:

Heirloom Love Confession

I understand that millions of Christians are
being persecuted around the world.
I also understand that, since I am a follower
of Jesus Christ, His new command requires me
to love, remember and, as able, help suffering
and persecuted fellow believers
in the household of faith.
I confess that I have not loved and remembered
my persecuted fellow believers in accordance
with the teachings and requirements of Scripture.
I will sincerely seek to change my ways and
practice biblical love for Christians who are
suffering and persecuted for their faith.

SIGN HERE

While working to abolish slavery throughout the British Empire, William Wilberforce challenged, "You may choose to look the other way but you can never say again that you did not know."

If you saw a gang of thugs brutally beating Jesus, would you intervene? If you knew Jesus was living in a squalid refugee camp—or a garbage dump—because those who hate Him had destroyed His home, how much of your abundance would you give up to provide Him food, shelter, clothing and medical care? If Jesus was on death row, about to be wrongfully executed for blasphemy, would you speak out for Him? Would you and your church mourn and cry out in an all-night prayer vigil for His release?

What would you do for Jesus?

Our King speaks today: "I tell you the truth, whatever you did for one of the least of these brothers of mine, you did for me" (Matthew 25:40).

Jesus is here today. He lives in North Korea, Sudan, Syria, Eritrea, China, Laos, Vietnam, Burma, Pakistan, Iran, Nigeria and India, where He is suffering at the hands of those who loathe Him. Millions of Jesus' followers in dozens of countries are bearing His reproach today. They are falsely accused, imprisoned, beaten, tortured, raped, enslaved and murdered every day. Are you grieved? Fervent in prayer? Giving sacrificially? Speaking out on their behalf?

We demonstrate our love for Jesus by our acts of compassion for the persecuted saints. The opposite is also true: We reject Jesus by failing to care for His suffering children. Jesus said, "I tell you the truth, whatever you did not do for one of the least of these, you did not do for me" (Matthew 25:45). And, "He who rejects you rejects me" (Luke 10:16). Many of us feel remorse when confronted with persecution news and our scriptural mandate to love one another. This is appropriate. It's a signal that we're in need of grace and change. Praise the Lord for His gracious mercy, expressed through John's reminder: "If we confess our sins, he is faithful and just and will forgive us our sins and purify us from all unrighteousness" (1 John 1:9). Let us each, if appropriate, come before the throne of grace and find fresh forgiveness. Then let us go and practice sincere love toward our suffering siblings.

May heirloom love—the love that Jesus taught, love from above—be preserved in our hearts. May we never be satisfied with the flavorless "love" that is from the world. May heirloom love flow through us and inspire others to turn to authentic Christianity.

Let us love one another just as Jesus has loved us.
Rescue those being led away to death;
hold back those staggering toward slaughter.
If you say, "But we knew nothing about this,"
does not he who weighs the heart perceive it?
Does not he who guards your life know it?
Will he not repay each person according to what he has done?

(Proverbs 24:11–12)

1. Whom will you love next? How? For how long?

2. Write down several ideas for goals your group might pursue togeth-
    er to continue to remember the persecuted.

Week Six

Day 6

Real Life in Nigeria

A YEAR IN MEMORIAM

As I read reports on suffering and persecution, I find myself struggling inwardly, torn between two realities: my life of freedom and comfort and the lives of my suffering brothers and sisters. How can these two realms exist at the same time on the same globe? What exactly does the Lord intend by granting me such privilege when others suffer such grief and tribulation?

For me this is a difficult but spiritually healthy struggle. By identifying with my persecuted brothers and sisters, I begin to identify and fellowship with Jesus in a way that might be available only to the persecuted and to those who choose to carry their burdens. It also provides me with much-needed reminders: that this is not my home, and I'm an alien here; that my hope is in the Lord—I look forward to His return and the city "whose architect and builder is God" (Hebrews 11:9–10). (In a very small but important way, it also helps prepare me for the surreal anti-Christian sentiment and growing backlash against Christians in the US.)

Please join me in the struggle. Let's experience and remember together one year—2012—in the death and difficult life of Christians in Nigeria. Let's memorialize the dead and stand with the faithful living.

BACKGROUND

Nigeria is home to nearly one-fourth of all sub-Saharan Africans. Its population is evenly divided between the Muslims, who are dominant in the North, and Christians, who form the majority in the South, with a belt across the middle equally mixed with both Christians and Muslims. Especially since 2009, Islamists have more and more boldly terrorized the northern and central states, sometimes killing Christian children, women and men by the hundreds.

The Fulani herdsmen and Boko Haram—linked to al-Qaida and the Taliban—are the Islamic groups responsible for most of the violence. They attack even fellow Muslims who don't practice the group's purist version of Islam. These two groups are not alone in this; many bloody incidents involve average Muslims continuing a decades-long history of deadly persecution of Nigerian Christians.

January: *Warning and Warfare*

On the second day of the New Year, Nigerian Christians awake to a published warning to leave the North within the next three days or face death. Christians are still reeling from Christmas attacks on churches in six northern and central cities. More than fifty were killed; the bereaved have only just buried their dead.

Hundreds of thousands of Christians have already fled their homes in the North, though most are indigenous to the region and feel they have nowhere else to go.

Thursday, January 5, Gombe state—The three-day deadline passes; the terrorists make good on their threat. A gunman bursts into a service at Deeper Life Church, kills six, including the pastor's wife, and injures at least eight. *Mubi town, Amadawa state*—At least four Christians are killed by gunmen.

Friday, January 6, Mubi, Amadawa—Christians gather at a town hall to mourn and plan funerals for those killed the day before; the same gunmen enter and kill at least seventeen. *Yola, Amadawa*—Masked gunmen kill ten at the Apostolic Church. *Borno state*—A Christian couple is murdered.

Across the North, hundreds flee.

Sunday, January 8 (estimated date), Bauchi—Terrorists use guns and machetes to massacre three Christian farmers on their farms.

Friday, January 20, Kano—Coordinated attacks on eight government locations, including four police stations, kill more than two hundred, reportedly because of terrorist suspects held in custody in the city.

Sunday, January 22, Bauchi—A Catholic church and an Evangelical church are bombed without casualties. A security checkpoint is attacked, killing two soldiers, a policeman and eight civilians, including seven Christians.

February: *"Simply Because It's a Church"*

Four straight days of violence start the month in northeastern Adamawa state. Islamists attack three different Churches of the Brethren on the first three days, and revisit the first one on February 4. Eight Christians and seven others are killed; three church buildings and numerous Christian homes are burned down. Christians fear attending services or even leaving their homes at night; some have had to close down their businesses. Fourteen of the denomination's pastors have been killed in Nigeria's violent Northeast, but the denomination president declares, "Hope is not lost. . . . A difficult situation cannot stop the Word of God."

A bombing of Christ Embassy church in northwestern Niger state on Sunday, February 19 injures five. On the following Sunday, Boko Haram claims responsibility for a suicide bombing in the Church of Christ in Jos, in central Plateau state; three Christians, including a toddler, are killed, and thirty-eight are injured. The Boko Haram spokesman says, "We attacked simply because it's a church and we can decide to attack any other church. We have just started."

March: *Words and Worse*

Captured Boko Haram leaders boast of their plan to "Islamize Nigeria" by taking down the current government, replacing it with Islamic law, and by attacking churches and any schools that don't "conform to our practice."

On Tuesday, March 6, Boko Haram attacks a Roman Catholic Church, a Church of the Brethren, a police station and a government building, killing at least two in Borno state. The following Sunday, a suicide car bomber targets a Catholic church in Jos, killing ten, including two boys, ages eight and sixteen.

April: *Sacrifices on the Altar*

Easter Sunday, April 8, holds unexpected terror for worshipers at All Nations Christian Assembly, Kaduna state. At least thirty-eight offer the greatest sacrifice; they fall victim to a suicide car bomber during service.

On Tuesday evening, April 24, a crowd of hundreds of Christians gather to watch soccer at a TV viewing center in Jos. A drive-by attacker throws an explosive device into the crowd, killing one.

And on April's last Sunday, gunmen on motorcycles throw explosives into a worship service at Bayero University, Kano state. They open fire on those fleeing the explosions, killing nineteen and wounding dozens, then riding away. Later the same day, in Borno state, gunmen enter the Church of Christ in Nigeria, killing the pastor and four others.

Nigerian Christians are urged to respond neither violently nor passively, but through "aggressive love," reaching out to help Muslim neighbors.

May: *No Greater Love*

On May 11, at the memorial service for the ten Catholics slain at the university, the bishop of Kano Diocese declares that persecution "should not weaken our resolve to remain faithful to Christ, but should make us strong."

In a sequence of terrorist attacks in fifteen Christian villages clustered in three regions of Plateau state, forty-four of our brothers and sisters lose their lives in horrific circumstances. Some are slashed and stabbed in their sleep with machetes and knives. Many children—including at least one infant killed with a machete—are among the dead. Dozens are injured and maimed. More than a thousand have either had their homes destroyed or are afraid to return to their homes; they take refuge where they can, many in schools, without food or medical care.

Worshippers persist in church attendance. Their defiant spirit is evidenced by "joyous bursts of singing" amid "bouts of fiery preaching and concentrated prayer."

June: *Fire and Darkness*

Boko Haram resurfaces for their busiest month since January, carrying out six coordinated attacks on three consecutive Sundays.

Sunday, June 3—Twenty-one are killed and forty-five injured in a car bomb attack on Living Faith Church and nearby Harvest Field Church, Bauchi state. One survivor reports hearing cries of members in the midst of darkness as fire engulfed the church. Tragically, eight of the deaths and twenty of the wounded are due to bullets fired by security forces into crowds of Christians who gather after the bombing to mourn their loved ones and to protest the government's inadequate protection.

Sunday, June 10—A suicide car bomber targets the Christ Chosen Church of God in Jos, killing four and injuring more than forty. The same day, gunmen open fire on worshippers inside the Church of the Brethren in Nigeria, Borno state, killing two and injuring several others.

Sunday, June 17—Three suicide car bombers attack three churches in Kaduna state—the Evangelical Church Winning All, Christ the King Catholic Church and Shalom Church. The blasts kill a total of more than fifty, including women, children and an army sergeant, and leave hundreds wounded—many so critically that the death toll is expected to rise.

July: *"I Enjoy Killing"*

On Saturday, July 7, Christians in twelve villages around Jos are terrorized when hundreds of armed attackers, some disguised in police uniforms, make their deadly way through the villages. Several hundred people have fled the violence and are homeless.

On that day, in the village of Maseh, some fifty members of the Church of Christ in Nigeria take refuge in their pastor's house, only to be trapped there and burned alive.

On Sunday afternoon, mourners on their way to a mass burial for Saturday's victims are attacked.

All told, the death toll for the weekend is more than one hundred, including two policemen and two legislators who had joined the funeral procession.

The following Tuesday, Pastor Ayo Oritsejafor, president of the Christian Association of Nigeria, testifies before a US House subcommittee, pleading with the US government to declare Boko Haram a terrorist organization. The group's leader, Abubakar Shekau, acknowledged individually as a terrorist by the US, has issued YouTube statements such as this: "I enjoy killing anyone that God commands me to kill—the way I enjoy killing chickens and rams."

August: *Death at Deeper Life*

On a Monday evening, August 6, worship is shattered when gunmen wielding Kalashnikov assault rifles surround Deeper Life Bible Church, Kogi state, and open fire. Reports indicate as many as twenty-five are killed, including a pastor.

September: *The Four and the Forty-Eight*

Four are killed—including a woman and a child—and more than forty-eight injured on Sunday, September 23, when a suicide car bomber detonates near congregants emerging from the first service at St. John's Catholic Cathedral Church in Bauchi.

The Nigerian faithful bury their dead.

October: *Hope Amid Horror*

The month begins with nighttime raids on three colleges. Attackers search room to room, sorting Christians from Muslims, killing as many as forty-five Christians by shooting them or slashing their throats. This happens in Mubi, Adamawa state, where Christians have suffered some form of violent attack nearly every day for eleven months.

CBN-TV declares Nigeria "a Christian killing field." Yet in the midst of the horror, reason for hope arises.

Even as Christians are being targeted for death, they pray for their enemies. And the Lord answers. One Boko Haram member reads the good news of Jesus Christ and comes to faith in Him. He witnesses to other members and miraculously still lives. Others see the "goodness of the Christian religion" in the lives of Jesus' followers, and although they're not ready to place their faith in Christ, they warn Christians of impending attacks.

On the last Sunday of the month a suicide bomber disguised as a Christian attacks St. Rita's Catholic Church in Kaduna, killing at least fifteen and injuring about 150 others. Inside, as people express their love to Jesus, they discover the building falling down on them. The archbishop of Kaduna Diocese grieves that 90 percent of the victims are children, yet he calls Christian youths to abandon all thought of reprisal.

November: *Ten Minutes Later*

On Sunday, November 25, worshippers are five minutes into their service at St. Andrew Military Protestant Church, Kaduna state. A bus loaded with explosives drives into the side of the building and explodes. More people gather to help the injured when, ten minutes later, another suicide bomber arrives and detonates his cargo, killing more than the first explosion.

December: *Holy Night*

In Yobe and Borno states, gunmen raid the Church of Christ in Nations and the First Baptist Church after midnight Christmas Eve services, slaughtering at least a dozen worshippers, including a pastor. Several Christian families are attacked in their homes.

Year end brings the confirmable number of Nigerian Christian martyrs for 2012 to more than nine hundred.

2013–Present: *Still Fatal, Yet Faithful*

The martyrdom of the Nigerian saints continues. And so does their relentless faith.[25]

* * *

Lament

Mourn with families left fatherless or motherless,
for the children who will never again
see that parent's smile or feel their hug.

Grieve with bereft mothers and fathers over the
murder of their children.
Heaven welcomes the young martyrs.
Sorrow for flocks who have lost their shepherds.

Share the burden of pain and restraint with
Christians who would seek vengeance.
Understand the fear and hatred with which
many struggle daily.
Pray for their purity and peace.

Learn faith, courage and perspective
from the Nigerian faithful.
Join in heartfelt appeal for the
salvation of the murderers.

Remember not only the dead,
but also the scarred and maimed,
the traumatized and the terrorized who live on.
Pray for their healing, both physically and spiritually.

"Don't be quiet.
Speak up to your government . . .
speak up to your church, support us."[26]

---

[25] Sources: Hundreds of reports from OpenDoorsUSA.org and Persecution.org.
[26] A published challenge from the Christian Association of Nigerian-Americans.

Week Six Group Discussion Guide

PRAY (10 minutes)

Share the latest persecution news stories. Then pray for your spiritual family in those true stories.

Ask the Lord to help you and your friends make plans to show the ongoing proof of your love for your suffering brothers and sisters.

SHARE (40 minutes)

Share with the group the personal commitments you've chosen in response to the following questions:

Day 1, questions 2 and 3

Day 2, question 1

Day 3, question 4

Day 4, questions 2, 3 and 4

Day 5, question 2

Discuss ways you can help each other remain faithful to these commitments in the coming months and years.

Share your thoughts about real life in Nigeria.

Persecuted?

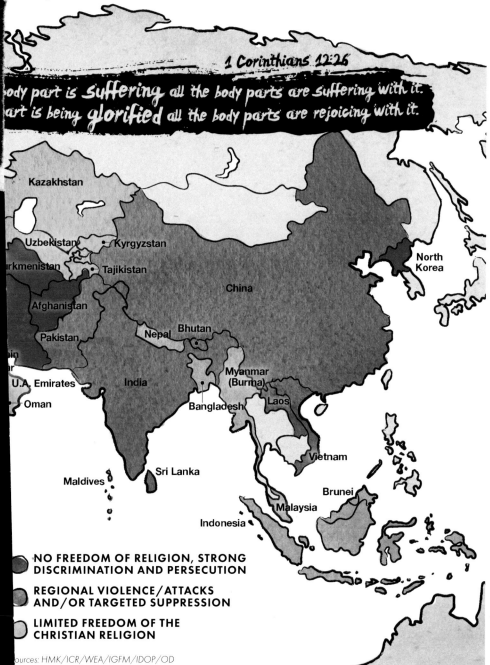

1 Corinthians 12:26

...ody part is **suffering** all the body parts are suffering with it.
...art is being **glorified** all the body parts are rejoicing with it.

Kazakhstan

Uzbekistan · Kyrgyzstan

rkmenistan · Tajikistan

North Korea

China

Afghanistan

Pakistan Nepal Bhutan

U.A. Emirates India Myanmar (Burma)

Oman Bangladesh Laos

Vietnam

Maldives Sri Lanka

Brunei

Malaysia

Indonesia

- NO FREEDOM OF RELIGION, STRONG DISCRIMINATION AND PERSECUTION
- REGIONAL VIOLENCE/ATTACKS AND/OR TARGETED SUPPRESSION
- LIMITED FREEDOM OF THE CHRISTIAN RELIGION

Sources: HMK/ICR/WEA/IGFM/IDOP/OD

A Call to Action

In 44 ICR Supported Countries, Regions

Afghanistan: Strengthen the underground Church. Provide health care and education.

Algeria: Train and support church planters and leaders. Networking and media ministry follow-up. Humanitarian aid. Church Planting in unreached ethnic group. Legal assistance for Christians.

Cambodia: Student lodging in Phnom Penh. Educational and material help for children living in slums.

"Caribbean": Support over 550 church planters and their families. Finance bicycles, and aid to hurricane victims. Acquiring titles for houses that can be used as churches. Thousands in underground Christian University.

China: Equip leaders of house churches with study and teaching material. Evangelistic camps for thousands of children and youth. Train teachers for children's Bible classes. Weekly children's Bible clubs in many provinces.

Egypt: Train and mentor leaders of large house church movement. Legal help and safe houses for persecuted Christians. Church planting. Micro-enterprise development; humanitarian aid.

India: Social work for outcasts and women. Reintegrate disabled. A school for children living in slums. Supporting 30 church planters. Provide legal assistance for six federal states and Christians facing heavy persecution.

Indonesia: Emergency aid for persecuted Christians. Equip around 300 pastors and workers with training. Children's ministry for several thousand children.

Iran: Provide assistance to persecuted Christians. Church planting and media. Provide Bibles and Christian literature. Aid with the goal of independence and selfsustainability. Leadership development.

Laos: Training church planters and leaders. Provide access to education for mountain area children. Develop income generating projects.

Libya: Support and train Christian leaders. Relief projects; training and networking.

Mauritania: Relief projects, church planting, economic support (micro enterprise development), help for persecuted Christians.

Morocco: Church planting. Relief projects for women. Youth ministry. Prayer initiatives. Media follow-up ministry.

Myanmar (Burma): Health clinics for the poor; cow-bank project. Production and distribution of Gospel DVDs. Training church leaders, connecting Christians, and running a boarding school for discriminated ethnic minorities.

North Korea: Care for refugees who fled to China. Work from home project for women. Access to Bibles, food and medicine. Feeding programs for the malnourished children in orphanages and daycares.

Pakistan: Medical and legal assistance for abused and wrongfully imprisoned Christians. Relocate Muslim background believers who are threatened by extremists. Support 24 church planters.

Sri Lanka: Legal assistance to persecuted Christians and churches under attack. Reconstruction of destroyed assembly venues. Support 15 church planters. Train 50 church staff and pastors in Bible theology.

Thailand: Jobs and education for refugees and children. Training church planters. Economic development for Christians. Rescue from human trafficking. Home for children with AIDS.

Tunisia: Relief projects, social networks, and media ministry follow-ups.

Vietnam: Assistance for persecuted Christians. Bible training for 100 Church leaders and 30 young Vietnamese Financial support for 100 church planters. Construction of assembly halls for churches.

REGIONS/ MULTIPLE COUNTRIES

Albania / Kosovo / Macedonia: Educational and material aid for children and poor families. Church planting, Christian radio programming, and village development project.

Central Asia: Mentor and train over 50 workers within house churches in predominantly Muslim regions. Aid for families of imprisoned Christians. Help pastors pay fines.

Horn of Africa: Assistance for Eritrean Christians in three Ethiopian refugee camps. Support and education for church planters. Support of persecuted Christians; Christian radio and TV programs.

Middle East / Arabian Peninsula: Mentor and help network the emerging indigenous churches. Leadership development and educational materials. Establish sustainable livelihoods. Safe houses. Active support of satellite television programs for the Arabic speaking world. Emergency humanitarian aid.

Russia / Moldavia / Ukraine: Relief goods and "Christmas parcel" project. Fund church building expansion. Produce Christian literature in Russian and Ukrainian. Prison Ministry and drug rehab programs. Aid for refugees. Translating the Bible into the Avar/ Avaric language (Dagestan in North Caucasus).

Syria / Iraq: Emergency humanitarian aid, rebuilding, and development aid for refugees. Safe houses. Help orphans and widows. Support many house churches. Leadership Training.

Turkic World (Countries from Bulgaria to China): Church Planting. Mentoring and connecting local Christians. Developing new and existing leaders. TV and media Projects.

Places like Nigeria, Israel, Madagascar and Colombia/ Venezuela are not mentioned. We cannot divulge sensitive information for security reasons.

ICR'S MISSION

"Providing spiritual and material assistance that enables persecuted Christians to proclaim the Gospel and plant churches in hostile countries."

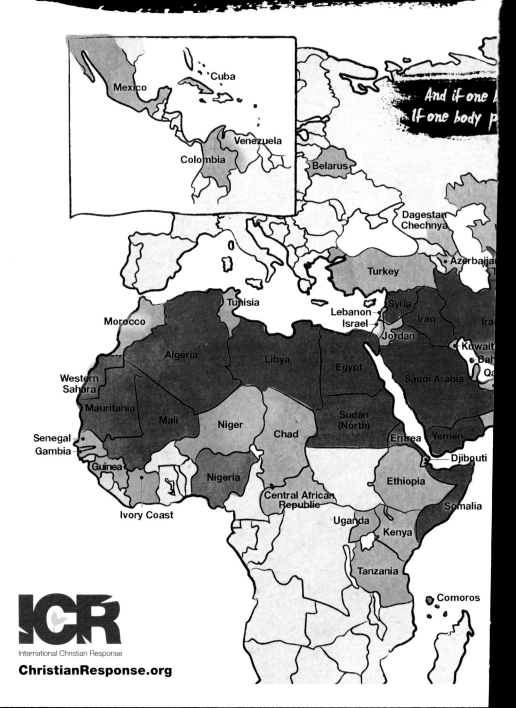

CLOSE (10 minutes)

Pray for the Christians in Nigeria. Ask the Lord to:

- Fill His children with bold confidence, perseverance and love, so their persecutors will be silenced and come to faith in Jesus.
- Protect Jesus' innocent followers from harm and provide for their physical needs.
- Bring surprising glory to Himself through the courageous witness of His people in Nigeria.

Pray for yourselves. Ask the Lord to bless and establish your intentions and plans to remember your faithful siblings who are in prison and affliction as though you are with them since you also are in the same body.

Appendix A

New Testament References to Money and Giving

GENERAL TEACHING

Matthew 2:11; 5:42; 6:19–24;13:7, 22; 13:44–46; 14:20; 15:5–6; 17:27; 21:12–13
Mark 1:44; 4:7, 18–19; 6:42–43;7:11–13; 11:15–17; 12:17; 12:41–44; 14:5–9
Luke 6:24–25; 6:30–36; 6:38; 8:7, 14; 14:33; 19:11–27; 19:45–46; 20:21–26; 21:1–4
John 2:14–16; 12:3–8
1 Timothy 6:5–11; 6:17–19
2 Timothy 3:2
Hebrews 11:4; 13:5
James 1:9–11; 4:3–4
Revelation 3:14–22

POOR, SUFFERING AND PERSECUTED SAINTS[27]

Matthew 24:42–51; 25:1–46
Luke 12:13–48; 15:1–32; 16:1–31

---

[27] Matthew 24:42–51; 25:1–46; and Luke 12:13–48 contain Jesus' teachings on money and judgment. Jesus directed these teachings toward those of us who have been entrusted with money and other resources (Matthew 24:45; Luke 12:41–42). In summary, He taught that those who have been so entrusted are responsible and accountable for feeding and caring for needy saints, whom He referred to as "the least of these" (Matthew 25:31–46).
Luke 15:1–32 and 16:1–31 contain Jesus' teachings on repentance from squandering money. Here Jesus teaches us how to use money correctly by caring for the least of the saints, such as Lazarus. The emphasis in this sermon is on repentance from selfish consumption (Luke 16:19) and on helping suffering saints (16:9) without specific reference to the cause of their suffering.
In my book *Prodigal's Progress: From Loving Money to Loving God* I present an in-depth consideration of these Scripture passages.

Acts 2:44–45; 4:32–37; 5:1–10;11:29–30
Romans: 12:8, 13; 15:26–28
1 Corinthians 16:1–4
2 Corinthians 8:1–24; 9:1–15
Galatians 2:9–10; 6:7–10
2 Timothy 1:15–18
James 1:27; 2:1–26; 5:1–6
1 John 3:10–24

THE POOR IN GENERAL

Matthew 6:1–4; 19:16–26; 23:23–28
Mark 10:17–31
Luke 10:30–37; 11:37–42; 14:13–14; 18:18–30; 19:1–10; 3:7–11
Acts 10:1–4, 31; 20:34–35
Ephesians 4:28

MISSIONARIES, GOSPELTEACHERS AND LEADERS

Matthew 10:9–10
Luke 8:3; 10:7
Romans 1:13; 15:24; 16:1–2
1 Corinthians 9:1–17; 16:5–6, 17
2 Corinthians 1:15–16; 11:7–9
Galatians 6:6
Philippians 2:29–30; 4:10–19
1 Thessalonians 5:12–13
2 Thessalonians 3:8–9
1 Timothy 5:17–18
2 Timothy 2:6
Titus 3:13
Philemon 1:7
1 Peter 5:2
3 John 1:5–8

Appendix B

By Grace Through Faith

If you were to read only the Scriptures quoted in this book concerning our responsibility to minister to suffering and persecuted Christians, you could get the impression that salvation can be earned by helping the least of the saints.

However, we know by reading the whole Bible that this is far from the truth. We must first be changed by God's grace, through faith, and then we can live in obedience to Him. The person who thinks that they can be saved from their sins by living righteously has confused cause and effect.

Take for example the following passage:

Then the King will say to those on his right, "Come, you who are blessed by my Father; take your inheritance, the kingdom prepared for you since the creation of the world. For I was hungry and you gave me something to eat, I was thirsty and you gave me something to drink. . . ."

Then the righteous will answer him, "Lord, when did we see you hungry and feed you, or thirsty and give you something to drink? . . ."

The King will reply, "I tell you the truth, whatever you did for one of the least of these brothers of mine, you did for me." (Matthew 25:34–40)

Some might read this teaching of Jesus and think that the "righteous" became righteous (and earned salvation) by serving needy people—that good works make a person righteous.

However, the Bible tells us clearly that one must be saved from his sins and be made righteous by an act of God alone—not by anything we can do. "A man is not justified by observing the law, but by faith in Jesus Christ" (Galatians 2:16).

Justification before God happens when one is born again, and this rebirth occurs by God's grace, through our faith. It's not earned by our good works. "It is by grace you have been saved, through faith—and this not from yourselves, it is the gift of God—not by works, so that no one can boast" (Ephesians 2:8–9).

It's God's gift of righteousness that transforms a person into someone who, by nature, does good works like serving the needy. Look at the very next verse in Ephesians 2: "For we are God's workmanship, created in Christ Jesus to do good works, which God prepared in advance for us to do" (2:10).

We aren't saved by good works; we're saved to do good works. A lifestyle of good works follows naturally in the life of a person who has been forgiven and made righteous by God. Through faith in Jesus Christ we're born again and become new creatures that will increasingly conform to the likeness of Jesus Christ (see 2 Corinthians 5:17, NASB; Romans 8:29).

The good deeds we do as we grow in the likeness of Jesus Christ are the effects of salvation and the proof that we've been saved. They're not the cause of our rebirth. Jesus said, "By this my Father is glorified, that you bear much fruit and so prove to be my disciples" (John 15:8, ESV).

Appendix C

Ministry Resource Guide

Disclaimer: This list is not comprehensive. My intent is to offer a starting point, to save you time and effort by identifying several organizations of which I am aware. I have little or no experience with many of these ministries, and I am not endorsing them. I urge you to carefully evaluate the integrity, work and effectiveness of these ministries before supporting them.

21st Century Wilberforce Initiative

ADF International

Barnabas Fund

China Aid

Christian Freedom International

Christian Post

Christian Broadcasting Network (CBN)

Christian Solidarity International

Christian Solidarity Worldwide

Christians in Crisis

Connecting Lives International Mission

Family Research Council

Global Response Network

Hardwired

Hudson Institute—Center for Religious Freedom

In Defense of Christians

International Christian Concern

International Christian Response

Institute on Religion and Democracy

Iraqi Christian Relief Council

Jubilee Campaign

Morning Star News

NK (North Korea) Missions

Nuba Reports

Open Doors

Philos Project

Religious Freedom Coalition

Religious Freedom Institute

Religious Liberty Partnership

Persecution Project Foundation

SHAI Fund

Voice of the Martyrs

Voice of the Persecuted

World Watch Monitor

Appendix D

Praying for the Persecuted Church

Here are some Scripture-based requests you can pray on behalf of our persecuted brothers and sisters:

1. Father, please help my suffering brothers and sisters to pay close attention to the truth, so they will not drift away from it (Hebrews 2:1).

2. Give them understanding of Jesus, the Apostle and High Priest of their confession. Help them emulate Him who was faithful to You, Father (3:1–2).

3. Grant them strength to hold fast their confidence and the hope in which they boast. Help them remain confident and hopeful to the very end (3:6, 14).

4. Lord, help your persecuted children carefully avoid an evil, unbelieving heart. Keep them from falling away from You, the living God (3:12).

5. Let them find encouragement in each other and in me day after day, as long as it is still called "Today," so that none of their hearts will be hardened by the deceitfulness of sin (3:13; 4:7).

6. Give them courage to hold fast their confession: "Jesus is Lord" (4:14).

7. Gracious King, keep my brothers and sisters mindful that your throne room is always open to them. Remind them daily to draw near with confidence to Your throne of grace, where they will receive Your mercy and find Your grace to help in their time of need (4:16).

8. Give them models in each other, whom they can imitate—bold fellow believers who, through faith and patience, will inherit Your promises (6:12).

9. Please encourage them powerfully to take hold of the hope set before them. Help them remember that You and your promises are faithful, so they might courageously confess their hope without wavering (6:18; 10:23).

10. Lord, teach them to draw near to You with sincere hearts in full assurance of faith (10:22).

11. Show them new ways to stimulate one another (and me) to love and good deeds (10:24).

12. Give Your persecuted children courage to keep assembling together and encouraging one another (10:25).

13. Please don't let them throw away their confidence, which has a great reward (10:35).

14. Father, grant them great endurance, so that when they have done Your will, they may receive what You have promised (10:36).

15. Strengthen their faith for the preserving of their souls, that they might not shrink back to destruction (10:39).

16. Help them lay aside every encumbrance and the sin which so easily entangles, that they might run with endurance the race set before them (12:1).

17. Lord Jesus, give them a clear vision of Yourself, and help them fix their eyes on You, the Author and Perfecter of our faith, who for the joy set before You endured the cross, despising the shame, and sat down at the right hand of Your Father's throne (12:2).

18. Jesus, you endured such hostility by sinners against Yourself. May my brothers and sisters consider Your example, so they will not grow weary and lose heart (12:3).

19. Some of Your suffering children have weak hands and feeble knees. Please give them strength and make straight paths for them, so the injured might not suffer more injury, but rather be healed (12:12–13).

20. Teach them to pursue peace with all people, and to seek Your sanctification, without which no one will see You (12:14).

21. Help them live up to the standard of Your grace toward each other. Prevent any bitter root from springing up and causing trouble and defilement (12:15).

22. Keep Your children blameless and innocent, like You, their Father—above reproach in the midst of a crooked and perverse generation, among whom they appear as lights in the world (Philippians 2:15).

23. Lord, strengthen them, and protect them from the evil one. Please rescue them from perverse and evil men (2 Thessalonians 3:1–3).

24. When they're called to speak for You, free them from worry about how to speak or what to say. Give them confidence that Your Spirit will give them the right words when they need them (Matthew 10:19–20).

25. Release them from fear of those who kill the body but are unable to kill the soul. Teach them instead the assuring fear of You, who are able to destroy both soul and body in hell (10:28).

26. Father, no sparrow falls to the ground apart from Your will. Remind your persecuted children of Your love, and that they're worth more than many sparrows (10:29–31).